Beginner's Guide to
ORCHIDS

Beginner's Guide to

ORCHIDS

GEOFFREY HANDS

Sterling Publishing Co., Inc.
New York

Creative director: Sarah King
Editor: Yvonne Worth
Project editor: Anna Southgate
Designer: Axis Design Editions

Library of Congress Cataloging-in-Publication Data Available

10   9   8   7   6   5   4   3   2   1

Published in 2003 by Sterling Publishing Co., Inc.
387 Park Avenue South, New York, N.Y. 10016

This book was designed and produced by
D&S Books Ltd
Kerswell, Parkham Ash,
Bideford, Devon, EX39 5PR

© 2003 D&S Books Ltd

Distributed in Canada by Sterling Publishing
C/o Canadian Manda Group,
One Atlantic Avenue, Suite 105
Toronto, Ontario, Canada M6K 3E7

Every effort has been made to ensure that all the
information in this book is accurate.
However, due to differing conditions, tools, and individual
skills, the publisher cannot be responsible for any injuries,
losses, and other damages which may result from the
use of the information in this book.

Printed in Singapore

Sterling ISBN 1-4027-0350-3

contents

introduction

Growing orchids is easy. Just buy a plant, place it somewhere suitable, like the bathroom windowsill, and water occasionally. What could be simpler? How can anyone write a whole book about it?

First, why the bathroom? Three reasons. The window glass is probably frosted, meaning less risk of burning tender leaves; it is usually comfortably warm, which most orchids likely to be grown by a hobbyist will enjoy; and often steamy, which means high humidity – and that will also make them feel at home. Not all orchids want all these things, but many do.

But, bathroom or not, what if the orchid does not flourish? The leaves turn yellow and fall off. Or, when the flowers are over, the plant does not grow a new leaf and never flowers again. Why not? How can it be woken up to do something positive?

And where else can they be grown – must it always be a bathroom?

Or suppose this first orchid awakens an interest, maybe it would be nice to have another one, a different one, and what different sorts are there?

ABOVE *Potinara* Burana Beauty – a cattleya hybrid

Maybe you are a bit of a perfectionist, and would like your orchid to have more flowers, or bigger and brighter flowers, and certainly to flower more often. Can this be done, and how?

This book aims to answer these questions. However, in trying to answer them it may provide more information than many hobbyists want, or indeed need. Just as an example, it is unnecessary to know how to provide pure water if the hobbyist is one of the majority who have a good supply available from the bathroom faucet. But this book will answer the question for the minority who have chlorinated, hard, or bad water.

In short, it is not necessary to aim for perfection in order to enjoy orchids, but many people who start with a liking for them, develop their interest and then want to grow them to perfection. Hopefully, this book will take them a good way along that road.

LEFT an attractively picotee-edged odontioda hybrid

OPPOSITE a so-far un-named odontoglossum hybrid bred from *Oda*. Florence Stirling

Orchids are different. They are special, mysterious, charismatic – the superlatives are endless. They are not like other plants. Their appeal reaches out to many who are not otherwise interested in flowers or plants. So little is known about them that inevitably many myths surround them. Some think that they are unattainable, out of reach, beyond the pocket of ordinary folk. And indeed that was once true, but now they are to be seen for sale in garden centers and supermarkets and at prices comparable to a few stems of roses or lilies. And this is for a living plant in flower. Inevitably the question is asked, "Are they not awfully difficult?" The honest answer is that if they are given quite unsuitable conditions then they are difficult, or even impossible, but if provided with the conditions they need, then they are perfectly tractable and will grow and flower every year for very many years indeed. And this is more than can be said for many other plants.

ABOVE AND LEFT a typical orchid flower – in this case

Burrageara Living Fire "Glowing Embers"

chapter **one** what is an orchid?

identifying an orchid

In the center of the lily flower is a rather stouter structure, extending as a continuation of the flower stem but above the petals. The free end of this forms the stigma. It has a sticky surface that is contacted by the pollen in fertilization. The stigma, ovary, and seeds before fertilization are, of course, the female part of the flower.

If the lily were to be converted by the wave of a magic wand into a typical orchid, one of the

LEFT a typical orchid flower, in this case *Odontoglossum cordatum*

BELOW a typical orchid flower, in this case *Odontocidium Crowborough*

How can you recognize an orchid? The best way of answering this is to compare a typical orchid flower with a typical non-orchid flower. Let us, for example, compare a lily flower with a typical orchid.

The lily has what the non-specialist will call six petals. If you examine it closely, you will see that three alternate petals lie slightly behind the other three and nearer to the stem carrying the flower. These rearward petals are, strictly speaking, sepals, not petals. Each of the true petals carries a number of filaments, called stamens, and each stamen ends in a pollen mass. (Lily pollen is often dark brown and powdery and stains clothing.) The pollen is the male sex part of the flower. With lilies the six "petals" are all very similar, but in many other flowers, the sepals are smaller than the petals, and may also be narrower and less brightly colored.

three petals would become the lip, or labellum. If the flower is in a vertical plane, the lip is usually the lowest of the petals. Often the lip is much bigger than the petals, sometimes it is differently colored, and often it is elaborated with lines, a crest, ridges, hairs, etc. It is, in fact, usually the landing platform for the preferred pollinator, maybe a bee or butterfly.

The ovary in the orchid lies behind the flower. However, there is a structure in the center of the flower, as in the lily, which is called the column.

Careful examination of this typical orchid will reveal that there are no stamens and – usually – no visible pollen. In fact, the pollen is hidden by

ABOVE showing the very small lip on a large vanda hybrid

ABOVE showing the small lip on a vanda type – actually an ascocenda hybrid

RIGHT *Masdevallia caudate*. The petals are the most striking part of the flower

BELOW *Masdevallia* Golden Trident. The petals are the most striking part of the flower

LEFT AND BELOW in slipper orchids there are only four parts of the flower to be seen. And, sometimes, if the lower (ventral) sepal is small, only three – *P. acmodontum* (left) and a typical hybrid (below)

the structure of the flower. It is carried on the column, but in a much less obvious way. The stigma is still present. It is also on the column, and again, is often not visible to the viewer.

These then are the essential characteristics of an orchid: no obvious stamens or pollen and three sepals that alternate around a flower with two petals and a lip.

However, there are some variations. It is worth pointing them out, even at this early stage, because orchids are so very variable in every respect – it is one of the interesting things about them. In vandas, the lip is quite small in relation to what can be very large petals and sepals. In the genus masdevallia, the lip is small and the petals are inconspicuous; it is the three sepals that are the striking part. And in the slipper orchids, only four, not five,

pollination

parts can be seen that might be called petals – arranged in the form of a cross – but the lip is turned into a pouch or slipper and lies in front of the lowest one of the petals.

Many orchids are arranged so that they can be pollinated only by a visit from one specific pollinator. For instance, there is an orchid found in Madagascar that requires a visit by a particular species of moth with a very long tongue – some 15 inches – that it carries coiled up. When the moth finds this particular flower, which is white and scented to help the moth find it in moonlight, it uncoils its tongue and inserts it into a 15-inch long spur at the back of the flower to reach the nectary at the far end. The moth gains nectar, but in doing so transfers pollen to exactly the right place, the pollen having been inadvertently collected from a previously visited flower. And as the moth withdraws its tongue and prepares to fly off in search of another identical flower, it collects the pollen from this flower, again inadvertently, and takes it with it. The scent is only apparent at night, because the moth does not fly by day.

One strange corollary of such specificity is that if the pollinator dies out, so does the orchid. Incidentally, this particular orchid was discovered way back in the days of Charles Darwin, who studied the pollination mechanism – a subject he was much interested in. That led him to predict the existence of what was then a quite unknown moth (to general scorn from disbelievers), which he said must exist for the orchid to be pollinated. Much later the moth was discovered, and given a Latin name meaning "as predicted."

The elaborate fertilization system provided by orchids means that, usually, they are not pollinated with their own pollen, although there are exceptions. It seems that this "out-breeding," rather than the kind of inbreeding that takes place in many other plants, where they are often pollinated with their own pollen, increases the likelihood of variation in the resultant seedlings. And in the course of geological time, when parts of a population become isolated from one another, the differences increase and develop and become significant enough for modern botanists to declare them a different species.

how they grow

Many, although not all, tropical and subtropical orchids are epiphytes. This word simply means "air plants." It refers to the fact that the plants live up in the air, perched on trees. They are not parasites. They take nothing from the host tree. They simply use the tree as a means of getting into the light, and perhaps also of escaping from the soil with its possible mineral contaminants. For although many other plants are tolerant of minerals in small quantities – there are of course exceptions – orchids seem to have less tolerance for contaminants than most plants.

Many epiphytic orchids will also grow on other surfaces if conditions are right. If they are growing

ABOVE dendrobium species on a tree in north Thailand

ABOVE *Dendrobium venustum* growing epiphytically on a stags-head fern in the rain forest

on rock, the technical term is lithophyte. If growing in the ground, they are called terrestrial. The term semi-terrestrial is sometimes used where plants are found growing in a kind of open litter formed of fallen branches and twigs with moss and other roots growing through. This distinguishes them from plants actually growing as true terrestrials in soil. The species *Dendrobium venustum*, for example, can be seen on at least one mountain range near Chiang Dao in Thailand growing on trees as an epiphyte, on the boulders below as a lithophyte, and occasionally in pockets of soil on the ground as a terrestrial. One large plant was seen growing epiphytically on a stags-head fern, which itself was growing lithophytically. Orchids are nothing if not adaptable, which is why it is possible for hobbyists to grow them in pots so easily.

One important feature is very nearly always present wherever an orchid is found growing in the wild, however it grows. This is free drainage, with a very ample supply of air to the roots. Epiphytes are quite extreme in both respects – and this is a point worth emphasizing. Orchids positively must have air around their roots.

species and hybrids

ABOVE *Phragmepedium besseae* remained undiscovered until very recently despite its bright color

The orchid family is one of the largest plant families. Experts differ as to exactly how many different species there are, but experts often differ as to whether two different species are in fact two species, or merely variants of a single species – which accounts for differences in the grand total. And then new species are still being discovered both in new areas and in quite well-known areas. One of the most remarkable of all slipper orchids (*Phragmepedium besseae*) was first discovered a mere 20 years ago, growing at the side of a main road in South America in an area well explored by botanists and orchid collectors for the previous hundred years – and it has bright red flowers a good few inches across. How it was missed so often is a mystery. An even more startling phragmepedium, with giant purple flowers, was reported in the press as a new discovery as late as summer 2002.

Give or take a few thousand, there may be 30,000 different orchid species. While some of these are to be found in temperate and even cold climate countries, the vast majority are in subtropical or tropical places where the diversity of plants of all kinds is greatest. It is these warmer-growing ones that provide the more spectacular or more interesting – or both – orchids that are the subject of this book. Indeed, it is these orchids that most folk think of when the word "orchid" is mentioned, at least in the absence of some additional qualifying words such as "native Florida," or "Mediterranean ground," etc.

Orchids were taken home by explorers from the earliest days, certainly by the first of the great European explorers in the 14th and 15th centuries, but it is probable that few survived both the rigors of a long journey in a sailing ship and then cultivation with an almost complete lack of factual information as to their needs. But knowledge slowly spread and by the 19th century at least, there were a number of collections of orchids in the gardens of some of the great estates in western Europe, and certainly in England, and experience was slowly being gained as to how to grow them. Inevitably, when success was gained, seed raising was tried, and what was more obvious than to apply pollen from one kind of orchid to a different kind of orchid – out of a spirit of scientific enquiry – and so the first man-made orchid hybrids were created.

One of the leading orchid firms of the day started a register of these hybrids, since continued by the Royal Horticultural Society of London (RHS). There had been well over 100,000 hybrids registered before the end of the 20th century, each a combination different from anything registered before. Thus, if pollen is taken from *Laelia crispa* and applied to *Cattleya maxima* the ensuing seedlings are named *Laeliocattleya amesiana* – the name registered by the original hybridist Veitch in 1884. If the cross is repeated today, the seedlings have the same name. And if the reverse cross is made, using the *Laelia crispa* as the seed parent and the *Cattleya maxima* as the pollen provider, again the same applies,

they are all LC (the recognized abbreviation for this man-made genus laeliocattleya). Proper usage gives a lower case initial for the species name, and upper case (a capital letter) for the hybrid name. If correctly applied, as it usually is in orchid journals and the better books on the subject, but alas not always by the trade, this is an important clue when looking at an unfamiliar name.

New hybrids are still being registered, in fact at a faster rate than ever before – amounting to several hundred every month. This does not mean that there are more than a hundred thousand different hybrids actually available to choose from. Many of the early registered ones would be hard or impossible to find, in the same way that many of the 30,000 species have never been collected and seed raised for hobbyists to buy and grow. But it does mean that, despite all the necessary qualifications, there is still an enormous choice of orchids available to those who search ordinary commercial sources, and an ever-widening range on offer in garden centers, and supermarkets.

It is also a curious fact that the price of orchids only ever goes down, not up. That is largely due to enormous improvements in propagation techniques and orchid culture generally, which became available in the closing years of last century and are now working their way through the trade and spreading ever faster and further around the world. The best practices in the beginning of this century have led to good large flowering plants being ready to leave the nursery about one year after small seedlings were first potted up, whereas 40 years ago only the best technique could achieve this in five years, and many took 10.

LEFT *Laeliocattleya* Doris "Pastorale"

ABOVE *Odontocidium* Crowborough "Plush"

In the first half of the 19th century when orchids were available only as wild plants, collected in the jungles of the tropics with enormous effort, and often at great danger, the rather small number of plants that survived the process were usually sold at auction – and the prices paid are quite unrecognizable today. A new variety – everyone wants something different – would fetch hundreds or even thousands of US dollars for a single plant. While it is difficult to convert prices into today's money, a housemaid in the castle of the Duke of Devonshire (who had a notable collection of orchids) would have been paid very much less than $150 for a year's work. Imagine paying a year's salary for one plant, or even 20 year's salary for one plant! It is easy to see why orchids were exclusively for the rich.

The discovery of the means of easy seed raising in the 1920s changed matters considerably. Even more significant was the discovery of tissue propagation in the 1960s. That enabled propagators to make identical copy plants that actually grow faster than seedlings. When this was coupled with great strides in culture, laboratory technique, and automated glasshouse controls in the years that followed the 1960s, it seemed that the prices of ever better orchids stayed static, while everything else, including average earnings, went up and up. In 1965, $25 for a plant would have seemed a very large sum to most people. Today, a price of $20 for that same plant would seem very little to most people. Hence orchids have gone from being the preserve of millionaires to being within the budget of all.

chapter two your first orchid

your first orchid

You have decided that you really must try an orchid. You have seen them in a local outlet and have been tempted, but so far resisted. But you argue (correctly) they are not that much more expensive than a good pot of African violets, or chrysanthemums, and you see other people buying them, so why shouldn't you. However, you do not know which to choose, and even if you like this color or shape more than that, how to pick the best plant from the several on offer? Or maybe you have been presented with your first orchid, possibly nameless, as is (regrettably) all too often the case with orchids in non-specialist outlets, such as supermarkets, garages, hardware stores, etc. Of course, you want to know what it is, and in both cases you want to know how to care for it, keep it, grow it successfully, make the flowers last as long as possible, and produce more flowers as soon as possible. Can you achieve all this? The answer is probably yes, but let's take it one step at a time.

We will start with a brief look at the 10 orchids most usually found in non-specialist retail outlets. However, the varieties available are increasing all the time, so if your orchid does not match any of these descriptions you will need to look in the gallery (see page 120) to find a description that matches the plant you have acquired.

ABOVE LC Gold-digger "Geoff's Own"

LEFT BLC Nugget AM/RHS

cattleyas

At one time, at least on the US side of the Atlantic, cattleyas were the most popular orchids – the ones everyone thought of when the word orchid was mentioned. Maybe they became too familiar and so went out of fashion to some extent, especially when breeders seemed intent on producing ever-larger corsage blooms. Modern breeders, however, are producing an ever-greater range of color and form in smaller flowers. Many are a few inches in spread, in vibrant colors, and have several flowers clustered on a stem. They will flower twice a year with indoor culture, and although already available from the specialist dealer, will surely find their way to the supermarket shelf as well before too long.

The name cattleya is often incorrectly used as an abbreviation for a whole series of inter-generic hybrids, which strictly speaking may be LCs BLCs, potinaras, kirscharas, and so on. The smaller flowered plants – the cluster bloomers – are compact, capable of producing two or three new growths all flowering at once without exceeding a 4–5 inch pot, and of doing well in brightly lit indoor situations. They like warmth, do not demand high humidity, and generally speaking are an obvious choice for indoor culture. The large corsage cattleyas come from a much larger plant, are unsuited to growth indoors, and are best kept for a large conservatory, or a specialist greenhouse.

RIGHT LC Doris Bush – a splash-petaled cattleya

cymbidiums

These are most likely to be available in late fall, winter, and early spring because they are particularly seasonal flowerers. A very few are summer flowering but they are not yet widespread enough to be a likely available plant. Cybidiums have lots of leaves, which are green and straplike, rather like a daffodil but much wider, typically 1–2 inches wide, and up to about 2 feet long. The leaves extend upward from a swelling, or bulb, sitting on compost, not below it as with a daffodil bulb. There are usually two to four flower spikes on a plant in a 5–6 inch pot. The spikes stand up as tall as the leaves but are clearly visible since they do not, or need not if staked, arch in the same way as the leaves. There may be as many as 20 or more flowers per stem. (Hobbyists always call an orchid flower stem a "spike.") The flowers are at least 2 inches across and possibly as much as 4 or 5 inches.

The color range includes whites, yellows, greens, browns, pinks, and near reds – hybridists have been trying to breed a bright red cymbidium, the color of a London bus, for more than a hundred years and will no doubt carry on trying. But this list of colors fails to capture the true magic of the actual color range. Moreover the lip is often of a different color, or has a band of another color – usually red – which contrasts well. Sometimes the lip is spotted in a different color. Mere words fail to due justice to a lovely flower.

Cymbidiums were at one time a favorite orchid with beginners, especially in cooler temperate regions, because they needed little winter heat. They are cool house orchids and will flourish in a temperature range of 50–80°F. Definitely one for those living in a cooler area, especially if the night temperature only rarely exceeds about 60°F. They do need cool nights in summer to initiate buds, and if kept too warm in a permanently heated apartment, may produce lots of new growths and leaves, but no flowers. As a result, some growers put them outside for the summer in cooler climes. In warmer places, such as southern California, better flowering has been successfully initiated by watering them at night with iced water for the few vital months of the summer.

One of the best things about cymbidiums is that the flowers can easily last for as long as 10 weeks on the plant, especially if it is not allowed to get too warm. In fact the cooler and shadier the plant is, the longer the flowers will last. This

RIGHT *Cymbidium* Red Brilliant

RIGHT C. Mini-Sarah with delightful clean colors

BOTTOM RIGHT *Cymbidium* Beacon "Red Torch"

BELOW *Cymbidium* Mimi "Lucifer"

means that cymbidiums are admirable as decorations for the foyer or hall. Cut flowers last for a few weeks or even a month, if picked while still fresh.

When buying a plant, look for clean, green, unblemished foliage, plump not shriveled bulbs, and if in flower, fresh flowers, preferably with some buds still to open – that way you know that the flowers have not been open for three months, and that you will get your money's worth in the first year. Ideally buy a plant where there is at least space to get a finger between the rim of the pot and any part of the plant, and then it will not need repotting this year. However, in real life, professional growers do not want to have to repot plants either, and so they time their plants to fill the pot and flower well at the point of sale. But do not despair, repotting is not that difficult, and is explained later in this book.

dendrobiums

You are likely to come across two kinds of dendrobium. Both have tall – anything from 6 to 12 inches – elongated, thickened stems called canes. One kind has leaves along the length of the canes (soft-caned), the other tends to have all the leaves at the upper end or tip (hard-caned). Their growing needs and flowering habits are different too.

The hard-caned ones need bright light and are happy to be warm all year – perhaps on a sunny windowsill, although take care that the plants do not bake. Flowers are produced in long spikes from the tip of the latest cane, often just about as the cane completes its growth. Well grown, with good light, a spike can have 10 or more flowers, even as many as 50 on some hybrids. Poorly grown in dimmer light, three or four flowers are more usual. They like more heat than cymbidiums.

The soft-caned ones usually have rather plumper and taller canes, with alternate and fleshier leaves along their length. They tend to like warmth in their growing season from spring to fall, but need a cooler spell, with a drop in temperature for a few weeks at some point in the winter, to give best results in flowering. Then they often flower in twos or threes from nodes over much of the length of the canes, sometimes including canes that are more than a year old – that is to say, the beautiful strong cane produced one year will not flower the following spring, but will flower a year later.

RIGHT *Dendrobium ochreatum*, another soft-cane type

ABOVE *Dendrobium* Halawa Beauty is a hard-cane type

ABOVE RIGHT *Dendrobium* New Guinea, a soft-cane type

RIGHT one of the tip-bearing hard-cane dendrobiums

In both types flowers will be 2–3 inches across, and come in a wide range of colors, including white, yellow, brown, orange, dark reds, and purple. Some modern breeds approach blue. Often there is a contrasting lip, which in some cases can have a dark, near black "eye." Other kinds have striped flowers. The range is very wide, and is still widening because there is an enormous genetic pool to draw on from well over a thousand different species. The indications to look for in choosing plants are similar to those in cymbidiums, except that the hard-caned kind may be ridged rather than plump. This is not an indication of a tired plant, merely a more mature one. There is little risk of a plant filling a pot and needing early repotting because the canes take up much less room than the fat bulbs of a cymbidium.

ABOVE *Dendrobium finlayanum*, has distinctively knobbly but soft canes and needs only a short rest in the fall

ABOVE *Dendrobium* topaz, from the island of New Guinea, needs rather more warmth than most.

RIGHT *D. fimbriatum* named for its wonderful lip , in the most usually seen variety "oculatum"

miltoniopsis

The so-called "pansy orchids," if labeled at all, are often called miltonias. This is, in fact, what they were called for much of the time they were grown, but botanists agreed to change the name, as botanists will, and mere hobbyists and orchid lovers can only follow suit. The flowers are not starry in shape, but nearer a disk and almost flat. They can easily be 4–5 inches in a vertical direction, and slightly less wide, with half a dozen carried on each spike. Each new growth and bulb of the plant produces two, three, or even more spikes.

The foliage of these "milts," as they are sometimes affectionately called, tends to be a silvery green, indicating a need for a fairly good light. Given a little too much light, the leaf color may have a pinkish flush. Otherwise they want eternal spring and love fresh air, a gentle humidity, as on a spring morning when the sun dries the dew, temperatures never falling far below about 60°F at night and never rising above 75°F by day. This may mean growing plants in a well-ventilated room, with open windows, or air-conditioning, depending on the location of the grower. But if grown in an air-conditioned room do watch humidity, for the air is often far too dry in such situations, and a means of adding water to the air will be needed (see page 65).

Although primarily summer flowering, a collection of a dozen plants will always have at least one in flower. Well grown, they tend to complete a cycle of growth, flower, and then start the next cycle in well under 12 months. With ideal conditions, twice-yearly flowering is possible. The color range is rather limited, from white through yellow to red and pink, but often with interesting and curious markings, called "masks," "waterfall effects," or "teardrops" depending on the imagination of the vendor. The masks are often black, making for very dramatic flowers. The flowers do not last in water if the spikes are cut, but remain good on the plant for several weeks. Usually, if there are several spikes they open slightly in succession so that the plants – as the orchid books published in the 19th century used to say – "last in beauty" for several months at a time.

Again, when buying, look for clean leaves and plump bulbs. Good plants have often started new growths at the same time as producing flower spikes. Vigorous, well-grown plants invariably produce two new growths from each old one.

LEFT an atypical 'milt' in that the mask is not contrasting – which makes a change!

LEFT a "waterfall" or "teardrop" pattern miltoniopsis

RIGHT M. Robin Hall x Cindy Kane

LEFT dark "masks" make these orchids dramatic

odontoglossums

This is a term used as an abbreviation – or even more abbreviated as "odonts." In fact, odontoglossum is one genus, but is related to many other genera so closely that hybrids can be made between two different genera – the so-called inter-generic hybrids. And those hybrids may be capable of being crossed with one another even when widely different in appearance and maybe even parentage. It all sounds easy, but in fact involves a great deal of breeders' skill and work. The end result, and continuing result, is the production of an enormous range of startling, beautiful, and fascinating plants. There seems no end to what can be produced, and new ones are still being bred, extending the range still further. Moreover, while most of the older "purebred" odontoglossums and odontiodas – those usually red-colored hybrids made by crossing large odonts with the tiny but colorful cochlioda – were essentially cool growing and could be difficult in slightly warmer conditions, some modern hybrids are happier that little bit warmer and are easy plants to flower. Some hybrids have been especially bred to be happy in even warmer conditions, such as those found in Florida or California.

ABOVE an old plain red odontioda – F.J. Hanbury

BELOW a modern miltassia hybrid with rich coloration, *Miltassia* Royal Diplomat.

Most have more or less similar growth habit, having bulbs typically larger than a hen's egg when seen from one angle, but flattened when viewed side on. There may be half a dozen leaves from the base clasping the bulb and perhaps one or two from the top. The bulbs are technically soft, usually plump not wrinkled or ridged. The straplike leaves are sufficiently flexible to wave in the air if there is a fan in the vicinity. Usually there will be a mass of about half a dozen bulbs on a flowering plant. Flower spikes are borne singly, or sometimes from both sides, emerging from between the leaves.

From there on it is difficult to generalize, except to say that the flowers will never be tiny – almost always an inch or more. Sometimes, if the flower shape is very starry, or even spidery, as distinct from round, it could be far more than six inches across from tip to tip. The spikes may extend from one to two feet, or much more on a big, well-grown plant. Not plants for a small Wardian case!

There will hardly ever be less than 10 flowers on a spike, and with smaller flowers 40 or 50 would not be uncommon. The color range goes from white, green, yellow, red – sometimes quite brilliant reds – to purples and browns. The flowers may be one color, or they may be blotched, spotted, or barred with other colors, or have petals of one color and a lip of a quite different color. The good thing about this group in general is that they will grow and flower on a cycle of rather less than 12 months, which means that a collection of these plants will always have something in flower.

Once more, look for clean foliage, plump bulbs, and hopefully some new growth. It is always worth selecting a plant with two or more growths starting from one bulb or growth – a sign of vigor.

BELOW LEFT *Wilsonara* Ravissement AM/RHS

ABOVE RIGHT *Oda* Chargia "Victor" with its blackcurrant coloration

BELOW *Wilsonara* Autumn "Intrepid"

ABOVE *Beallara* Tahoma Glacier – odontoglossum breeding for warmer growing

LEFT *Beallara* Witches Cauldron "Magic Brew"

oncidiums

This genus is closely related to odontoglossum – often there is some oncidium ancestry in the multi-generic plants discussed above, especially the warmth tolerating ones. But purebred oncidiums are often found. These typically have a cloud of yellow flowers, perhaps with touches of red, brown, or green somewhere on each flower. The flowers are smaller than odonts, but to compensate, spikes of 50 plus flowers are the norm. These plants have harder bulbs and often ridged, and rather more leathery foliage – all indicating an ability to withstand higher temperatures, and perhaps a need for more light. Many oncidiums have a mildly climbing habit – in the wild they are epiphytic, growing on trees, and tend to produce each new growth slightly above the last one, perhaps in an attempt to get near to the light that they need. This may necessitate more frequent repotting than with some other plants, so when choosing a plant look to see that the flowering bulb is not already far above the compost, as this may dictate an early repotting.

LEFT a typical pure-bred oncidium, often sold under the fanciful name "dancing ladies," which has no authenticity, botanically or horticulturally

BELOW showing just one flower from perhaps a hundred on the spike of *Oncidiujm wentworthianum*

BOTTOM LEFT one of the "*variegata*" oncidiums, which are very small plants, originating from the West Indies

BOTTOM a typical "dancing ladies" oncidium

paphiopedilums

This is the principle genus of slipper orchids for most purposes. One other important slipper genus is cyprepedium, but they are still very hard to come by, and also difficult to flower, often needing a specific spell of very low temperatures in order to succeed. For this reason they are not included here, apart from mentioning that if you consult old orchid books, such as the rather fine ones with wonderful engravings, produced in the late 19th century, you will find many "cyprepediums" described. However, these have since had their name changed by botanists, and are now called paphiopedilums. Aficionados of the slipper – and their cultivation is quite a cult – call them "paphs."

TOP LEFT Odontoglossum Geyser Gold

ABOVE Miltonidium Summer Fantasy "Waikiki Sunrise"

ABOVE P. Pisar "Perfection"

LEFT Paphiopedilum Transvaal "Asjah" AM/SAOS

Many of the species, of which there are just under a hundred different kinds, are quite easy orchids, liking relatively low light levels and a stable temperature very similar to that in which the hobbyist is likely to be comfortable. While most of these slippers only have a single flower per growth, and only once on that growth, they are sufficiently free with their new growths, and the flowers last such a long time – sometimes many months – as to make up for that. There are two groups that have more than a single flower. The successional flowerers bear one flower for a few weeks, and after that falls, another bud will develop on the same spike, and so on, sometimes for as many as 30 successive flowers over several years. The true multi-florals bear several flowers all open at once on one spike. This group includes some with awesomely large and magnificent flowers, often very dramatically colored. One type, for example, has black stripes on a yellow ground.

A final bonus with some paphs is the lovely foliage, in several shades of green, from almost silver blue to a dark green, which may be almost black, in a mottled pattern, making them handsome plants even when out of flower.

Perhaps surprisingly, since these plants have no storage bulbs, tubers, or rhizome to speak of, merely tufts of leaves, many paphs are epiphytes. They are found on trees, and some have a tendency to climb. So, when buying, look out for

RIGHT a multi-floral where all the flowers are open together

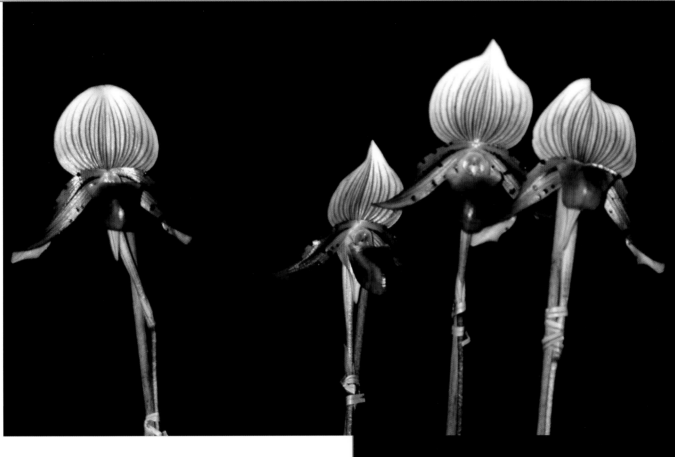

growths well above the compost, and avoid them until you are confident about repotting. This is not difficult, but perhaps not ideal for an absolute beginner making a first purchase. Paphs, however, are easy to repot (see page 99). They really love being repotted, usually responding with a burst of new growth.

TOP one of the parents of this novelty hybrid is *P.venustum* which has passed lovely foliage on to its progeny

RIGHT a successional flowering hybrid

phalaenopsis

Plants in this genus are often affectionately called "phallys." They are the houseplants *par excellence*. It is possible to buy a plant in flower and enjoy flowers for at least six months in the first year just by keeping the plant alive. You may even do better than that if the plant actually grows, producing new leaves. Phallys like the warmth of a cozy apartment, and they appreciate steamy bathrooms, but will make do with substitute humidity, for example from a few associated foliage plants – maidenhair ferns are good for this. They do not demand brightness, and the light levels found inside a reasonably lit room are perfectly acceptable to them.

Usually a 4–5 inch pot is enough for a flowering size plant, which will then have up to three pairs of leaves, typically as long as 9 inches. The flower spike may be 18 –24 inches long with a row of near circular flowers up to 4 inches across, or even more in some fine varieties, in a range of colors. There are whites, whites with orange or red lips, pinks (including plain, spotted, and striped), yellows, and a range of hot "desert" colors. Breeders are working on green and also purple phallys.

A very well grown mature plant in ideal surroundings can have 30 or even more flowers, which will be arranged along the main spike in two rows – facing both ways – and also along three or four branches. More usually, when indoors, or because a plant is not strong enough to carry all those flowers, the branches do not develop immediately. Instead, the spike produces

ABOVE once, phalaenopsis colors were always plain, but modern breeding produces "different" flowers

LEFT one of the so called "art shades" flowers

maybe 10 flowers at the top. When those flowers are over, if the spike is cut off below the last fallen flower (not at the base of the spike near the leaves, which would be the obvious thing to do), and above the point where a branch would have developed, the plant will often develop the branch after a few weeks, and a second flowering period will begin. Sometimes, the second and third branch can be induced to develop and flower in turn. The site of the branches can easily be seen as a small bract or leaflet clasping the stem.

If the plant was not strong enough to carry all those flowers at once, it was almost certainly not strong enough to go on growing a new leaf at the same time, so sooner or later the spike will have to be cut down low to allow the plant to grow. But, as mentioned, its needs are easily met indoors, and after the first spike is cut at the lowest point possible, the plant will grow a new leaf, and then start a new spike. By the way, if the plant already has half a dozen leaves, it is likely to lose the lowermost leaf as the new one develops – they very rarely get more than six, although good culture will produce longer, thicker, and broader leaves – and likely more flowers at one time, at the next flowering.

ABOVE A good white phalaenopsis takes some beating as a plant for any occasion
RIGHT Phalaenopsis spike with branches developed from the nodes on the main stem

Phalaenopsis are not seasonal, and although there may be more flowers at one time than another, it is not hard to have at least one plant in flower all the year from a few plants.

Since phallys have no bulbs you will need to examine the foliage. Most phallys will have rather stiff leaves if well grown. In fact, they can be so stiff that it may seem they will crack across if an attempt is made to flex them. Leaves that are stiff may be the ideal, but are not often seen. However, avoid plants with floppy leaves. It almost certainly indicates an absence of good live roots, or that the plant has been too long in the store without attention, resulting in desiccation that has probably damaged the plant – permanently. You may buy such a plant cheaply, and if given plenty of loving care it may recover, but it will be at least a couple of years before it has grown a fresh set of roots and approaches being as good as the plant you could have bought. And the word used is "may" not "will."

ABOVE this kind of pattern is known as "French spotting" – maybe it first appeared on a Paris-bred hybrid ?

vandas

While the word orchid meant a cattleya to most people in North America – and still does in South America – vandas and their allies are the most common and spectacular orchids in the East, especially in Thailand and southeast Asia generally. While many Europeans and North Americans admired their large and lovely flowers, most hobbyists thought that they could not be grown successfully. Nowadays it is becoming better understood that there is nothing very different about their needs, although they require rather more light than some other orchids. Their needs are generally similar to those of cattleyas, which have long been grown successfully, so there is no real problem about growing them.

Again the name is used as an abbreviation for a whole group of related genera and their inter-generic hybrids. In general, pure "straight" vandas have large blooms and tend to be blue – an unusual color in orchids – or purple, red, yellow, white, or green. Blues and reds or mixtures of the two colors are the norm. The hybrids made with other genera, such as ascocendas, are often yellow, orange, or shades derived from those colors, with much smaller flowers, and many more of them. Not plants for the indoor grower, because of their light needs as well as their size, but wonderful plants for the outdoor grower in warmer climes, and great plants for the greenhouse. Often considered to be summer flowering, they do in fact flower several times a year given appropriate treatment.

ABOVE *Vanda* Chindavat x Gordon Dillon

ABOVE a miniature vanda cross with a lot of ascocentrum in its make-up

ABOVE *Ascocenda* Gua Chia Long "Leopard"

ABOVE LEFT the most famous vanda hybrid, and the easiest to grow – *V. Rothschildiana*

ABOVE RIGHT a typical "blue" vanda

RIGHT *Vanda* Valse Bleue

ABOVE a different kind of vanda, called "terete," with leaves and stems like green knitting needles. This one is famous – *V.* Miss Joaquin

zygopetalums

One of the species of this popular genus (sometimes sold as *Z. mackayii*) produces 3–4-inch flowers with thick, waxy petals, which means that they last well, and have the bonus of a delicious perfume, similar to that of hyacinths. Add to that the general dimensions of the plant, which are fairly compact, the freedom with which new growths are thrown up, so that the plant with one flowering spike this spring may produce two next spring, and more again thereafter, and the unusual coloring of a nearly blue lip and green and brown petals, and the species already sounds like a winner. It was hybridized for years, without producing anything much different, maybe due to some dominant genes, but in very recent years some good new ones have started to emerge, with sometimes near black petals, sometimes all green, and most recently some pink variants. There is also a look-alike, which is actually a propetalum, where the distinctive shape of the zygo is kept — those dominant genes again — but the yellow color of the other parent (the relatively diminutive promenea) comes through. You will need to keep a good lookout for this one, but it can be found in retail outlets from time to time.

Zygos have bulbs like moderate-sized plums, and straplike foliage. Flowers are produced out of the side of new growths. If the plants suffer, the bulbs do not seem to shrivel, but the foliage will. Zygos seem to be able to keep roots live and active for more years than most orchids — 3 or 4 years is normally the maximum — and they do best when this possibility is exploited. That means very good culture, and such a plant can be recognized by the fact that the oldest bulbs still have all their leaves. Once the roots have been lost from the oldest bulb, the leaves on that bulb will turn brown and fall off, although the bulb may remain green and plump for some years thereafter. But the bulb is not contributing much, if anything, to the general well-being of the plant, once that has happened.

The roots are particularly vulnerable to bruising in repotting. Therefore do not choose a plant that is about to outgrow its pot and will soon need repotting, for the beginner may not see flowers again for several years.

ABOVE a zygopetalum hybrid

points to consider

There are a couple of other points to watch out for in making purchases of plants before gaining experience. First, some supermarkets like to sell orchids in ornamental pots, sometimes of glass, glazed ceramic, or even galvanized iron, without any drainage holes. They say this is to avoid spoiling the furniture when the plant is watered, or that such a container is beautiful in its own right. But these pots are likely to prove fatal to the plants when they are watered, for they will drown. Orchids, above all other plants, must have air around their roots. If such a plant is purchased, or obtained, a very early repotting is a must. One solution is to put the plant into a plain flowerpot with normal drainage holes, water, drain, and then place that pot in the ornamental container, removing it from time to time when further watering is to be carried out.

And second, plants past their sell-by date that have spent too long in the store, over-heated and under-watered, and now flagging and sickly, do not make good buys, however cheap they are. It can take years to return them to good health. In those years they demand the same effort and space as a good healthy plant — or even more — but make no return. In fact, they may die despite all that is done. If you want a serious challenge, that's all well and good. If you want to grow orchids and see flowers, avoid cheap "bargains."

understanding the jargon

Orchids rarely have common names. Even when they do, they are not very helpful. For example, a spider orchid may be a Mediterranean ground orchid with flowers less than one inch across, a plant from Australia with flowers three inches across, or a brassia from the South American rain forest with even larger flowers. All of these are totally different to one another in shape, color, and everything else. Latin names are necessary if everyone is to know what plant is being discussed.

Every wild, naturally occurring plant has a name made up of (usually) two words in the international system first devised by the great Swedish naturalist Linneaus many years ago. The same system is also applied to man-made hybrids. The first word is the name of the genus (plural genera). The second is the species, or specific plant in the genus. The specific names are meant to be descriptive, but sometimes the description may not be very helpful. For example, *Cattleya lawrenceana* is just "Sir Trevor Lawrence's cattleya," *Laelia gracilis* is "the graceful

laelia," and so on. Each genus includes a number of species that botanists think are fairly closely related to one another, or at least more closely than to plants in other genera. There can be just one species in a genus, or a great many, such as the 1,000 plus dendrobiums, or the 80 or 90 paphiopedilums.

ABOVE Brassia lawrenceana cv. "longissima" where the petals are much longer than in the ordinary forms of B.lawrenceana.

ABOVE a fine color form – *Odontoglossum bictoniense* "Lyoth Pearl" AM, but the plant has now had its name changed by botanists

A great number of genera are collected together into the family — orchids are just one family among many. But since it is such a large family, maybe the largest in the plant kingdom, it is further divided up. First, all the slipper orchids form one division composed of just four genera, but they are different from all the others in certain important respects, for example, they have exposed "naked" pollen. All of the other orchids form the other division of the family. But since this is still a very large number of genera, the division is further divided into tribes, following the same principle that all genera in one tribe are rather more closely related to one another than they are to any in another tribe.

As scientific knowledge increases, sometimes botanists agree that a particular plant ought not to be in the genus where it has been placed, but in another one, and so the name gets changed, to the irritation of all growers who have been accustomed to a particular name. This is why many — but not all— old cyprepedium names are now paphiopedilums, and *Odontoglossum bictoniense* is now *Lemboglossum bictoniense* — if not changed again to something else — and so on.

Usually, when a hybrid can be made from two species that are not in the same genus (which is quite unusual outside the orchids, and quite common in the orchids), it is invariably between species in two genera within the same tribe and not between orchids in different tribes.

When the two plants belong to different genera it makes an inter-generic cross. In fact, when this is first done between two genera, a new genus is created. Breeders are allowed to

ABOVE *Potinara* Yuan Gold — with parentage derived from four different genera

name the new genus according to an internationally agreed set of rules. Originally new names were created out of the parent names — thus a cattleya (abbreviation C) crossed with a laelia (L) made a laelocattleya (LC). A brassovola crossed with a laelocattleya makes a brassolaelocattleya (BLC). But when a sophronitis — which is yet another genus closely related to these three — was crossed on to that, it all became too much, and the result was called a potinara (abbreviation "pot"). Since those early crosses more than a hundred years ago breeders have become even more adventurous and incorporated genes from as many as seven or eight genera into a single hybrid.

A third name sometimes appears on a plant label. Often this is a "cultivar" name, when someone has a plant that is thought to be distinguished in some way. For example, one plant of *Cymbidium alexanderi* was found to be tetraploid (doubled chromosomes) and had especially fine flowers. This was called "Westonbirt" after the home of the owner. It is a cultivar of *Cym. alexanderi* and was at one time the most important cymbidium for breeding purposes.

Generally speaking, a Latin name indicates a species, but in the early days of name registration for hybrids, imitation Latin names were allowed, such as *P. shillianum*. This is no longer allowable in new registrations.

awarded plants

The old-established horticultural societies of the world mostly have some kind of award system. When an award is conferred it means that a committee of experts has sat in judgment, and according to the quite artificial and arbitrary standards that they employ, the plant in question has been found to be of merit. This almost always means exceptional flower quality. The commoner awards are Award of Merit (AM), the higher (highest level) First Class Certificate (FCC), and the lower HCC for highly commended. Not all of these bodies use the same names, and generally each has its own unique award, which others do not recognize. Usually, to get an award, a flower has to be larger and rounder than previously seen for an orchid of that particular kind or breeding. But the way the rather illogical system works is that representatives of a newly discovered species also get awards, just because they are new, and particularly fine orchids do not get awards because they are not supposed to be as good as ones (long since dead and gone) that the records claim existed a hundred years ago. An awarded plant is always given a cultivar name by its proud owner to distinguish it from other members of the same species or hybrid grex. All hybrids having the same name form a single grex.

A once awarded orchid is, and all the divisions made from it are, still entitled to "wear their honors" by adding the letters after the name, thus *P. Maudiae* "Magnificum" FCC/RHS, even although a hundred years have gone by and standards have moved on since that award. Maybe logic suggests that a complete listing of an award should be HCC/AOS/1955 – and then the would-be purchaser of a plant would know that if state of the art breeding was wanted, this is not the plant required! Of course, for most hobbyists, none of this matters.

RIGHT *P. Maudiae* "Magnificum" FCC/RHS

monopodials and sympodials – patterns of growth

ABOVE showing the habit of a phalaenopsis developing two flower spikes

There are two basic patterns of growth in orchids. The simplest is where the plant has a single stem, or tuft of leaves, and as the plant grows the stem elongates, or the tuft produces new leaves – year after year and season after season – without apparently ever reaching finality. Plants like this are called monopodial, meaning single growth plants. There are several eyes or nodes associated with each length of stem between successive leaves (often invisible) and each node has the ability to develop into a root, or a flower spike, or even a replacement growing point should the main growing point be damaged. Most of these nodes never develop into anything, but they seem to keep the ability in reserve, as long as the stem is sound. A plant growing up a tree trunk, getting ever higher, or for that matter a plant in a pot, growing ever taller, may eventually die off at the lower part, without affecting the viability of the upper part, and those unused nodes perish with the oldest stem. The "stem" is sometimes quite clearly visible, that is, the successive leaves may be well spaced, and sometimes it is not so visible, as with phalaenopsis, where the leaves are so close together as to show no stem between them. But it is there, nonetheless.

Flowers of monopodial orchids are produced from lateral spikes. This means that if an orchid, which appears to be a monopodial, produces a flower spike at the tip or apex, it is not a monopodial at all, but a sympodial that just happens to have only grown so far. Phalaenopsis can be unintentionally induced to produce a terminal flower spike by injudicious spraying with some insecticides. When they have done this, they can grow no further, and although they can remain alive for many years, they will not flower again. Monopodial spikes are from nodes, so that in plants where the interleaf stem portion is short, they appear to come from the leaf axils. Occasionally a monopodial will produce a second or further growths as "keikis." These are adventitious plants, produced from nodes, or even on flower stems, that in time will develop their own roots, and indeed can then be taken off and established as separate plants or left on to grow a rather jungly mass of a plant. *Keiki*, by the way, is a Hawaiian word that is now recognized by hobbyists worldwide. A few monopodials also branch. Each branch then behaves in the same way, potentially growing forever.

eventually, and hopefully, one or more branch growths develop. This can make the plant look as though it is a sympodial orchid. The monopodial habit seems to be an extreme case of "apical dominance" – the apex of the plant, the growing tip, is the most important part of the plant and receives all the hormones, etc, necessary for new growth at the expense of the rest of the plant, although of course roots and flowers develop lower down.

BELOW a keiki on an old phalaenopsis spike

ABOVE RIGHT a reed stem epidendrum flowering from the apex of a growth

LEFT a phalaenopsis, showing a newly emerging flower spike

Monopodials can be difficult to recognize as such when they have developed into a bushy mass of growths. However, this rarely happens, except with quite mature plants growing in ideal surroundings, such as an undisturbed wild plant in its native location. What does happen in cultivation, which again can make recognition difficult, is that the growing point of the plant is destroyed. This may be because of bacterial rot caused by water remaining in the center of the growth for too long without ever drying up. The plant can continue to look healthy, but it will stop growing until

This technical aspect of apical dominance can be exploited in order to propagate certain monopodials. The plant is deliberately upset and positioned in a horizontal mode instead of vertically – turning the plant through 90 degrees. The tip is no longer the top, or in other words, every leaf node is uppermost. This encourages new growths to develop from the nodes that are already there, and as the new growths develop their own roots they can be taken off and established. Some southeast Asian nurseries sell what they call "top cuttings" of vandas that have been developed this way. Notable monopodials are phalaenopsis, vandas, and angraecums.

ABOVE showing branching growth. The oldest, small, bulb had two growths each of which have made a much larger bulb and both of which now have two new growths each, although

sympodials

sympodials – meaning side-by-side, as in sympathy, symphony, etc. – produce a growth seasonally. They usually complete that growth, and then start another at the side of the first, a further one at the side of the second, and so on. A strong plant will start two growths from the previous one at the same time, although some kinds of orchid are much better at this than others. For example, a reasonably grown cymbidium will easily move from one initial growth to produce two new growths at the same time, and within half a dozen years there can be a potful with new growths everywhere, and of course each new growth carries its own possibilities of flowers. Experienced growers select plants of sympodial orchids, when making new purchases, by looking to see how many new growths exist. The plant with two new growths has potentially twice as many flowers next time around, or alternatively, is already on the way to being divided to make two separate plants, each with its own new leading growth and chance of flowering.

In general each growth has only one opportunity of flowering – there are a few, but only a few exceptions to this – and if the growth does not flower at that time it never will. It is as though there is a switch somewhere that is "on" from the time the growth starts, but goes to "off" as soon as the next growth starts. Sometimes, it is true, the flower spike will be first seen after the new growth has appeared, but almost certainly initiation and the first steps of development started earlier. The main exceptions in terms of more than one window of opportunity for flowering are dendrobiums, where some are able to flower for several years in succession from the same cane, certain masdevallias, especially those that produce several flowers on a single stem, which is of triangular cross-section ("triquetrous masdevallias"), and a few other orchids where the spike actually carries more bud potential than the plant can handle at one time, as in phalaenopsis (see page 48).

Some epidendrums are called reed-stem types for the obvious reason that each new growth is like a reed — a thin pencil-like stem furnished with alternative leaves (one on one side, and the next one above that on the opposite side, and so on). These end in a flower spike at the tip when the cane or growth is tall enough and mature. Occasionally, the flower spike will produce branches with further flowers after the main crop has fallen, although some just go on lengthening the spike and can always have 20–30 flowers out, with new ones opening as old ones fall, not just for months on end, but even for years on end. Eventually, or on a stronger plant rather sooner, a new growth will arise from the base of the plant, or as an adventitious growth partway along the stem, or both. In nature, that is to say in the wild, these plants often form a scrambling mass growing through shrubs, and those adventitious growths help the plant gain height and a new direction. In cultivation it is certainly tidier, and often more convenient generally to take off the keikis and pot them up separately, but it is good to put several in a single pot — and maybe get several growths all flowering together in a year or two.

ABOVE *Cymbidium* Gareth "Everglades" is a so-called miniature, with flowers less than 3 inches across — miniature only when compared to "standard" cymbidiums

RIGHT *Epidendrum o'brienianum* , a reed-stem orchid which can flower for years on end, with new buds continually forming in the center as the spike extends

ABOVE showing the oldest leafless backbulbs at the front, and the new growth at the back. Note that the size has increased year-by-year, growth-by-growth

With sympodial orchids, it is easy for the grower to see how his or her culture is progressing. There is a permanent and obvious record in the way each growth represents either the result of one single year or at least one season or set of seasons (since some orchids, especially members of the odontoglossum alliance, can complete a growth and flowering cycle and start another in rather less than 12 months). Are there more new growths this year than last? Are this year's growths larger than last year's? If so, all well and good, if not, why not? And even with very little experience it is not necessary to wait for a year or two to see how the plant is progressing. Just look at the width of the newly emerging growth – if it is going to make one bigger than last time, the leaves will start off looking as though they will be wider. With monopodials it is, of course, more difficult, and often they tend to make leaves of exactly the same size whether they are growing well or not. It is just that when growing well they make them a lot quicker, and hence make more in a season, and have a greater potential for flowering as a consequence. So with orchids of this class (monopodials), in order to see how well you are doing some kind of discreet marking may be useful, such as a tiny ink mark on a leaf to show where the plant had got to at a particular time. This will enable you to compare growth rates year by year, or month by month.

bulbs, canes, reed-stems, and others

Many sympodial orchids produce bulbs. Botanists say that they are not true bulbs at all, for a true bulb has layers like an onion. Orchids have pseudo-bulbs without layers. In general, hobbyists agree, but only the pedantic use the full term; most just carry on calling them bulbs. They usually extend above the compost, rather than below (if they are below they are more likely called tubers). In comparing the culture of one year with another, or one plant with another, it is, of course, bulb size that will be compared. Bulbs are of many different shapes, according to the kind of orchid. Sometimes covered with the scars of old leaf bases, sometimes not, again depending on kind. If the "bulbs" are tall and thin, they may be called canes, especially if they have actual leaves, and not just leaf-bases along their length. If the canes are slender and leafy all along their length they make reed-stems. In such a large family it is hardly surprising that there is great diversity in vegetative parts, just as there is in most other parts.

Flowers may appear either at the tip or apex of the growth, as they do with many but not all cattleyas, as well as reed-stem epidendrums, or from the center of the completed growth, as in slipper orchids. With others, the flower spike appears out of the center of the newly developing growth, as in pleione and many coelogyne, or from the side of the completed growth, as in odontoglossums. There are some orchids, including representatives of some of the just-mentioned genera, which produce special flowering shoots (not connected with a new growth at all) from a rhizome interconnecting the bulbs or growths.

It is the roots of an orchid which are worthy of most consideration, and which are perhaps most different from the similar parts of other plants. In the first place, orchid roots are almost always surprisingly thick for a herbaceous plant, that is, not a tree. Next, root hairs are only rarely present. The appearance is most typically white but with green tips. The white part is called velamen, and is rather like blotting paper in having an ability to take up water. Often the whole root will turn green when thoroughly wet, and then return to white as the water is passed into the plant and the air refills the cells of the velamen. The green tip is the growing point, indicating that the root is healthy and still extending. No green tips, no new root action – the plant is resting. In some genera, the roots can be as much as one-quarter or one-third inch thick. Even on quite small, tufty plants they are often more than a sixteenth of an inch, maybe an eighth of an inch thick. Most orchids have roots

ABOVE phalaenopsis grows well in these near-transparent pots, allowing the roots to be seen

that will branch or ramify, but a few will not, notably masdevallias. This means that if masdevallia root tips are damaged, those roots do not continue to extend – they cannot branch off somewhere and start again. Since masdevallias also seem to produce all of the new roots at only one particular point in the growing cycle of a new leaf (these plants have no distinct bulb, and although there is a special term for their stems – ramicaule – most hobbyists call each separate growth "a new leaf"), the plant suffers a severe setback and has to await new growths before new roots can be produced.

On the other hand cymbidium roots are so freely produced that, in repotting, it is possible to shorten all the existing roots drastically in order to suit the new pot, confident that these shortened roots will soon branch and grow again.

The appearance of the plant can be a guide to its cultural requirements, and an indication of how far its needs are being met.

Many aerial roots (e.g. vandas) mean that the plant needs and expects some considerable atmospheric humidity to sustain it, especially during notional "dry" seasons. Bear in mind that a dry season in a place where the total rainfall is measured in yards rather than inches, may mean a light shower each week or two, rather than pouring rain for an hour or two every day. In other places, the words can be taken more literally! However, few orchids, except terrestrials, which intentionally drop their leaves and go dormant for a few months, can do without refreshment from humid air, dew, condensation, or actual rain for very long.

Large bulbs almost certainly mean that the plant has reserves to carry it through drier portions of the year, and the harder those bulbs are (admittedly a difficult thing to tell) the more likelihood that the plant expects a drought period. Not that it is essential, as indicated by the large-bulbed cymbidiums, which are very happy to go on growing all the year around, and hence will need watering and feeding all the year around. Try missing out watering altogether, as a sadistic experiment, and it may be quite surprising just how many weeks or even months the cymbidium can survive before the bulbs start to shrivel (but having shriveled they may not recover quickly, so the experiment is not recommended on your best plant!).

Soft bulbs that are plump and unshriveled, even on the older parts of the plants, with no ridging or wrinkling, indicate a plant used to having its water requirements met very frequently — maybe a plant from the cloud forest. Such a plant needs high, or even very high, humidity at all times. In the wild, such a plant may be bathed in a mist — often chilly — almost every night and sometimes all day too. Additional watering into the pot is not a substitute. Plants without bulbs at all must also have regular water and are unlikely to appreciate much of a dry rest. Slipper orchids are in this category.

Leaves with a silver color usually indicate a tolerance of high (good) light. Dark green leaves, on the other hand, almost certainly mean a plant grown in dim light, but not necessarily a plant that demands it. For most orchids with green leaves, a leaf color as green as some apples is probably right. And if apples can be many shades of green, then so can orchids, according to variety, and only experience will tell which is right. Observation is the basis to learning.

A reddish flush to the leaves often means too much light and incipient sunburn, although some paphs, by way of example, naturally have purple streaks or marks on their leaves, especially the undersides.

BELOW a miltoniopsis, in this case M. *Faribole* "Elisabeth"

flower quality

ABOVE orchid flowers can be green – *Coelogyne meyerian*

The most important attribute of flowers is that they are liked. Beauty is in the eye of the beholder. The hobbyist with good sense, and there are no other hobbyists, will select plants that he or she personally likes and appreciates, although diplomatic growers will add a plant to their collection if it is admired by their partner to please the loved one even if it's not quite their personal choice.

But you may desire to show off a plant, perhaps to take it to the local orchid society and place it on their plant table at the monthly meeting, or even "put it up" for consideration for an award. What do experts consider a good flower? Some of the considerations will be the same as those anyone is likely to apply, although it must be remembered that flowers to be shown must be fresh, clean and actual – none of the "it was better than this last time it flowered" or "you should have seen it last week." Judges have to judge what they can see, and nothing else. Clean colors, well-held flowers, nicely spaced on the stem, all pointing in the same direction (if appropriate for the variety) and a good clean, tidy, well-presented plant all play a part. Otherwise, the ideal set is usually a large flower for the kind, of good substance – waxy rather than tissue-papery – with wide petals so that the whole flower is more like a disk than a star. Obviously this depends on kind.

Some orchids, such as brassias, have long and narrow petals – they are sometimes called spider orchids as a consequence – and no brassia flower will ever be called disk shaped. But even so, one with, say, half-inch wide petals is better than one with narrower petals. In some genera, the petals should overlap so that there is no gap or "window" between them – phalaenopsis and cattleya certainly come to mind here.

However, the novice grower need not worry about such matters when showing, and can expect a warm welcome for joining in at all. Confidence will come with practice, and knowledge gained will soon enable the grower to reach a personal opinion about whether an orchid is worth showing. No show organizer is likely to object to an extra entry!

chapter four where to grow orchids

culture

Windowsill or dining table? This question implies a single plant, or maybe a very small number, unless it is a very large window. With orchids in general there is always the need to approximate as closely as possible the conditions that they have evolved to accept. If it is a hybrid, while it is likely to be easier to please, it is still the ancestral species that dictates the plant's needs. In general, humidity is the most difficult condition to provide indoors. Outdoors, except in desert places, a humidity of 60 percent is perfectly normal – rising at dusk, and in places where there is dew (from condensation) to 100 percent at some time in the night, and then falling again after dawn as the sun rises, unless it is raining. Indoors humidity may be much lower. Low humidity places a stress on orchids, as they will then transpire moisture faster than the roots can replace it. Humidity can be

ABOVE a well-flowered masdevallia

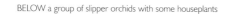

BELOW a group of slipper orchids with some houseplants

improved by localized spraying – it is not necessary to soak the furniture, merely a gentle puff with something like a scent spray – but not, of course, Chanel No.5! Water is the stuff to use. But this will need doing quite frequently and simpler means are possible. One is to associate the orchid with a few houseplants, which will themselves transpire water – breathing it out of their leaves, and thus creating a microclimate of greater humidity around the orchid. Ferns are very good for this, and maidenhair ferns seem to associate particularly well with orchids, their delicate foliage showing off the orchid flowers to some advantage. The ferns, or whatever, can be watered rather more heavily to make up for their water loss, without harming the orchid. Another possibility, which may be combined with the added houseplants trick, is to stand all the plants on a water tray. Hide the open water with some gravel or pebbles, and lift the base of the pots out of the water, so that foot rot does not result – the ensuing evaporation will do the trick. It may be a surprise how often it is necessary to top up the tray.

Light is difficult indoors. A south window or a south-facing room has the best light, but a position near the glass may be a recipe for baked orchid. Some orchids will stand it, but a careful choice is needed, and even then they should not be too near the glass. Paphs will often do well on north windows, and east or west ones may be useful in giving some light, without too much risk of burning. But the difference between one window and another, even of the same aspect, can be enormous and it may be necessary to try out a potentially suitable plant in one place, and watch it carefully, being ready to move it the moment it starts to look unhappy.

It will be obvious that a plant needing a cool rest in order to flower cannot be grown in a continuously warm room. If you like cool-growing masdevallias, or cymbidiums, or any of the dendrobiums – all of which need a cool rest in order to flower – somewhere appropriate must be found, or you need to give up on the idea of growing these plants. Consider the possibility of using a spare room solely for the rest time, sometimes as short as a few weeks, when you could turn down the thermostat. Few orchids will complain too much if all of their needs are not met all of the time, as long as most of their needs are met for most of the time. But the best culture, for those aiming for perfection, does need a closer approximation to ideal conditions.

ABOVE a mixed collection of orchids and houseplants decorating a room

BELOW a group of miltonia orchids with some houseplants

the next step up

If there are more than a few plants, a windowsill will not hold them all. The next step is the dedicated enclosed indoor area, which may be a Wardian case, or in modern-day terms, a light-cart, or more ambitiously, a growing room. Wardian cases were miniature greenhouses used to carry plants on sailing ships in the 19th century so as to keep them alive on long journeys. Effectively, what you want is an enclosure, where you can control temperature and humidity, in particular, and perhaps light too, and separate the contents from the rest of the room. Usually the enclosure is treated rather like an ornamental aquarium, in that it is stocked with especially suitable plants, and probably specially lit to show them off. There are other similarities between fish-keeping and orchid-growing; fish-keepers suppliers are a useful source of

ABOVE *Sievekingia fimbriata* is a very rare plant from Costa Rica, but can be found in cultivation by assiduous searching

equipment and materials for this kind of operation. In fact, an aquarium can be used as a Wardian case.

Obviously, for a small enclosure, Wardian case, or light-cart, you should choose plants that are ornamental, even when out of flower. Think of the more attractively leaved paphs and jewel orchids (anoechtochilus, goodyera, etc.) and/or ones with clusters of small, bright flowers – such as the smaller cattleya hybrids, some of which can be induced to flower twice a year in these conditions. Many people like pleurothallids, which have the benefit of flowering even more frequently in suitable conditions. Some of those with quite tiny flowers can be very beautiful when well grown and completely covered with flowers. Moreover, plants in tiny pots can be quite full sized and reach specimen size quite quickly – no waiting until the plant fills a six-inch pot before it flowers.

LEFT *Pleurothallis immersa* – well-flowered miniatures can be captivating

location

There are many locations inside a house that will be comfortable for people and also suit some orchids, but, even so, adjustments may be necessary for the plants. Strangely enough it may be easier to provide ideal conditions for orchids if the growing room is not permanently heated to the temperatures many people prefer in their rooms. Or, at least, it will be easier to provide the conditions good for any particular range of orchids if there is a free hand in this respect.

ABOVE a disa hybrid useful for the brilliance of their flowers

LEFT a modern disa, with stunning color, and a big flower too, often four inches across

BELOW one of the varietal forms of *Disa uniflora* showing that latin names must not always be taken too literally

Clearly the first thing to do is to decide which orchids you want to grow. As explained earlier, orchids are rather crudely classified according to the minimum nighttime temperature needful for good growth. The usual classifications, covering maybe 90 percent of orchids likely to be grown, are: cool, intermediate, and warm. There are 5 °F differences between each of these groups. The normally accepted figures for minimum, winter, and night temperatures are 50, 55, and 60 °F respectively. These figures should not be thought of solely as the minimum that the plants would tolerate without harm, in the sense that warmer temperatures may be harmless or even better. These are the average temperatures needed at night for the good of the plant, or in some cases, in order for flowering to be induced. So if the growing room has temperatures outside the appropriate range at night, heating or cooling may be called for if the orchids are to do well. Otherwise, choose different orchids!

ABOVE *Spathoglottis guinensis* comes from West Africa

LEFT *Bollea violacea*

OPPOSITE PAGE the yellow form of *Disa kewensis*. Yellow disas occur but do not set seed in the wild, however the hybridist can make them do this.

ABOVE *Angraecum leonis* – white-flowered

plants are often night scented too

LEFT an un-named hybrid disa from South Africa,

where much of the work on this group is being done

temperature

If heating is to be provided for the growing room – which for convenience we will call the orchid room – it may be from the main system of the house or apartment, a radiator with its own thermostatic control, or maybe an independent heater. If there is no convenient heating system to tap into, electric fan heaters are fine, but their output should not be directed against the plants for that would desiccate them. If the plants are on a table or bench, direct the heater below the bench or, better, away from the bench so that the warmth gently fills the space. Other possibilities, especially if the orchid room is away from the main house in a garage or outbuilding, may involve a fuel heater of some kind. If flame is involved it is very desirable that exhaust products should be isolated from the growing space. Some horticultural heaters are advertised as being good for plants because of the carbon dioxide in their exhaust, and while it is true that all plants need this, traces of noxious gases in the fumes, which might be harmless to other plants, can be fatal to orchids. Ideally, if you are using any appliance with a flame, there should be an exhaust flue leading out of the space, and an inlet for combustion air leading into the space. Some more sophisticated heaters have a so-called balanced flue that does both, and also uses heat from the exhaust to pre-heat the incoming air.

The best control of all will allow for a daytime temperature and a different nighttime one, which is lower. The technical term for this is diurnal shift. A difference of 5 °F is the minimum to be useful, and much larger differences are better, providing the minimum and maximum acceptable temperatures are not exceeded.

If temperatures are likely to be above the maximum at any time, cooling may have to be considered. There are room air-conditioners, for example, but if the cooling is needed simply because of sunlight, shading, or insulation, extractor fans might offer a solution.

One way or another, the room should be controlled so as to give the desired minimum nighttime temperature in the middle of winter, slightly higher nighttime temperatures as the season advances, month by month, until past midsummer, then reducing again until midwinter. Midsummer temperatures at night may be 10–15 °F higher than midwinter ones. Daytime temperatures should be higher than nighttime, and again a difference of say 10–15 °F is useful.

The significance of maximum temperatures is that plant growth speeds up as the temperature rises to a peak determined by the metabolism of the plant, but falls if that peak temperature is exceeded. Just as all plant growth ceases below a specific minimum temperature, so it does above a higher specific figure. Generally speaking, no orchid is growing much above 85–90 °F – plants adapted to very hot places usually rest in the hot season and grow in the cool season. Of course, the reverse applies in places where it is rarely hot and more frequently cold – a situation surprisingly frequent in the tropics, where orchids grow because they are at high elevations in the mountains and often in quite windy places too. Even near the equator there can be permanent snow on high mountains, and many orchids come from quite high altitudes, even if not actually near the snowline.

One of the very interesting possibilities of an orchid room is that the season within the room can be under the control of the grower. It can be eternal spring, or midwinter, in March – if the heating/cooling and one or two other factors are appropriately controlled. This provides endless opportunities for growing seasonal orchids, and for producing blooms at times to suit the grower.

lighting

Having got the temperature under control, lighting is the next factor. It is unlikely that the indoor orchid room has adequate lighting, unless it is a glass structure such as a sunroom, conservatory, or maybe studio. In any of these cases, light control by way of shading may be necessary, as well as for cooling, but since this is a more likely problem in a greenhouse it will be discussed later (see page 69).

Otherwise, you will have to consider supplementary lighting. Where artificial lighting is used, some non-obvious considerations apply. The heat from bright lights can scorch plants – a 500-watt spotlight produces half a kilowatt, which will roast a plant within reach! Low-voltage lighting (halogen) can give bright light – although brilliant light is unlikely to be needed anyway – without risk of burning. If ordinary fluorescent tubes are employed (use a mixture of warm white and cool white, or No.74 spectrum for most purposes), they may have to be within a few inches of the leaves (less than a foot) to provide enough illumination for growth. If in doubt use a light meter – 2,000 foot candles (22k lux) as a reading at leaf level is right for many orchids, less for dim-light lovers – maybe even down to less than a hundred for jewel orchids. Levels above 4,000 are not often needed for any orchid.

A good approximation of light value can be obtained by using a good-quality camera and a sheet of good white matte (not glossy) paper placed where the orchid is to be. Set the camera to a film speed of 25ASA, and a shutter speed of 1/60th second. An indicated lens aperture of f4 will show a light value of 1000 lux, and pro rata, that is, with the same aperture and shutter, a film speed of 50ASA would mean 2000 lux, a shutter speed of 1/125 second would mean 4000 lux, and so on. If in doubt, ask a camera buff to help out. It will be understood that if maximum daylight value is in question, the readings should be taken in sunshine in the middle of the day in midsummer, and so on.

In a completely dedicated orchid room do consider the interesting opportunity of growing on several levels. There is no reason at all why every plant should be on a table. Consider shelves, one above the other, each with its own light – but make sure that water from the upper shelf cannot reach the lower shelves, and at all times remember that water and electricity together can make a fatal combination. If a professional electrician is called in to do the installation and wiring, make sure that he or she understands just what is intended by way of splashing water around and spraying, so that appropriate waterproof fittings can be specified. They can be expensive, but are likely to cost less than a good funeral.

Air movement is important to the health of plants, almost to the point that the more there is, the better – perhaps short of providing gale-force conditions. Static air is stale air. Without some movement, the plant will take up all the carbon dioxide available from the air immediately next to the leaves, and it will not be quickly replenished. As a result, the plant lacks an adequate supply of an essential requirement. If the air is moved around, this will not occur. Whatever it may be, almost any plant looks better when there is a fan in operation.

BELOW *Oda Keighleyensis*. A hybrid first made over a century ago, but still worth growing. Likes it coolish

humidity

Humidity can be difficult in an orchid room. The desirable level for orchids is likely to be 60–70 percent relative humidity, as measured with a hygrometer. Be warned that cheap hygrometers (hair hygrometers) are rarely accurate for very long, although they can be recalibrated by wrapping them in a wet towel for two hours and then zeroing at 100 percent. The most efficient cheaper kind is a wet and dry bulb thermometer, where two parallel thermometers give different readings – one reads the air temperature and the other the temperature of water fed from a little bottle via a wick. In 100 percent humidity there is no difference between readings, but in drier air there is an increasing difference in the two readings according to temperature. Compare the two readings against a table, which is supplied with the equipment, but is also available in textbooks, since it is a standard and nothing to do with the manufacturer.

BELOW *Restrepia antennifera* is a pleurothallid miniature suitable for a growing case

It does seem that low levels of humidity cause stress in orchids, which reduces as the humidity rises. However, if it rises too high, the stress may be minimal but bacteria and fungal infections flourish freely. For instance, white flowers will develop black spots very quickly. Aim for 60–70 percent and a happy medium is provided. Of course, remember that what is being measured is relative humidity – as the temperature rises, the humidity falls, and vice versa. If 60 percent is provided in mid-morning, it will fall, unavoidably and without it being a cause for concern, to lower figures at midday, and rise to higher figures by night – providing the temperature is similarly rising and falling – which is desirable, necessary, and natural. The point is to try and recreate natural conditions in the orchid room.

How to create an increase in humidity, or if necessary reduce it, is another matter. Essentially, an increase requires more water in the air. In a suitable situation water can be poured on the floor. In a more sophisticated set up, ground-level sprays distribute water at periodic intervals, controlled by a pump on a timer, or from a water main with a timer-controlled supply valve, such as a solenoid valve. In an even more sophisticated version, this is controlled not by a timer but by a hygrostat. However, none of these is likely to be a useful suggestion if a spare bedroom is converted to an orchid room.

Water can be put into the air in the form of what the makers call "cold steam" by an electronic humidifier. Suitable models can humidify up to 500 or 1,000 cubic feet, and have a tank that can be filled with a few gallons of

ABOVE kefersteina, a little grown genus from the South American rain forests, has several unusual orchids which can be show stoppers when well flowered

BELOW a complete plant of a restrepia in a mere 3 inch pot

water so as to be self-sufficient for a few days at a time – depending on circumstances. Even larger models, called hydrofoggers, can be connected to the mains water supply and an electric supply. Quite a large volume of air – even amounting to some thousands of cubic feet – can be filled with fog after relatively few minutes running. How often rehumidification will be required depends upon how fast the moisture is lost. In practice, this means how much ventilation is provided. It is probably sufficient to rehumidify during the nighttime hours, when it is cooler, and less ventilation is needed to dissipate the humid air, then allow the humidity to fall in daylight, without attempting to rectify it. This after all, is entirely natural, and what happens, albeit to a less degree, in the wild.

ventilation

This brings us round to the last factor to be considered after heat, light, and humidity. There is something about fresh air, which makes it different to stale air, and it seems that plants can tell the difference, just as people can. Many plants seem to grow better outdoors rather than indoors, even when all other factors seem to be the same. It is also been observed that, in an enclosure, plants do better when the enclosure is large – the larger the better – for several reasons.

Green plants take the carbon dioxide out of air, and this is almost universally present all round the globe at about the same percentage. Plants utilize the carbon, turning it into sugars with the addition of hydrogen and oxygen from water, through the process called photosynthesis, which is carried out by chlorophyll. They then get rid of the surplus oxygen. Under normal conditions the increase in oxygen and decrease in carbon dioxide is never noticed in a place where plants are grown because there is continuous mixing and replacement, any more than an increase in carbon dioxide and a shortage of oxygen is noticed in a house or apartment occupied by people but no plants. Every time a door or window is opened air moves through the opening, and even if all the doors and windows are shut there is still a quite surprising amount of air movement.

But, nevertheless, some ventilation is a good thing if it can possibly be provided – for plants just as much as for people. Depending on internal and external conditions ventilation can be used to allow warmer air in – instead of heating – or warmer air out, instead of cooling. If neither is necessary but ventilation is possible, then an hour or so of open ventilator to completely change the air is desirable, at least once a day.

LEFT hybrid odontoglossums can be very variable, even from a single seed-pod, with different patterns on the flowers

a shade-house or greenhouse

ABOVE vandas grown as bedding plants in Singapore. When too tall they are cut down with a hedge trimmer, and the prunings pushed into the ground to grow on as cuttings

This is merely an externally located growing room, albeit one probably devoted to plants and nothing else. It may be, and very desirably is, devoted solely to orchids, in which case it may be glorified by the name of orchid house. And if it is not, initially, devoted solely to orchids, it probably will be sooner or later, since orchid growing is nothing if not addictive, and the African violets, tomatoes, bananas, or whatever that fill it up will soon find themselves shouldered out. Even to have read this far demonstrates that you are probably already hooked on a serious obsession that can last for life, and will provide endless pleasure, interest, frustration, and satisfaction.

A shade-house will be required in tropical situations, perhaps to grow native orchids (ones coming from the locality) and provide conditions at ground level that are approximately similar to those at treetop level in the wilds. Anyone living in such a place – a land where tropical orchids are native – potentially has access to both plants and information about their growing conditions, which is simply not available to growers in the non-orchid parts of the world, such as in northern parts of America, Europe, southern parts of Australia, etc. (And all that can be said, is that hobbyists in these other cooler places may have nothing but envy for the tropical orchid grower.) The shade-house will only perhaps need a covering to protect plants from falling leaves and twigs from surrounding vegetation and from birds. And maybe nothing special needs to be done by way of providing heat or light, humidity, or limiting temperatures. In other matters such as pests, plant selection, etc., the novice tropical grower may find help elsewhere in this book, but has little need to read the rest of this section on outdoor orchid houses.

A greenhouse, where conditions inside are controlled to be different from those outside, must be managed to provide the required conditions. Much of what is written about conditions indoors in Wardian cases, or orchid rooms applies here. The special problems of a greenhouse are

RIGHT large-flowered vandas in a shade-house in Thailand.

BELOW complex paph breeding – P. Martha Torrance "Doris"

primarily to provide enough light in the winter, especially at a latitude where days are short in the winter, but long in the summer – as distinct from the tropics where they are of similar length all the year – and to avoid likely overheating in the summer, which could cause scorch. This comes from excess temperature at the leaves rather than too much light, although reducing light is one way of avoiding it. But if the reason scorch occurs is understood, it will also be realized that keeping the humidity up, and keeping the air movement going will minimize the risk. But, especially if clear glass is used for glazing the orchid house, light, and consequently heat, may have to be restricted and any of three practical measures are likely to be useful.

First, shading can be applied in the form of a whitewash on the glass. The disadvantage is that it contaminates rain falling on the glass and may make it unsuitable for collection and use in watering the plants. This may be unimportant, but see page 89 before deciding.

Green (usually) shade cloth is made for commercial use both as a shade material and as a windbreak. Often it is listed in terms of the light reduction – 40 percent, 50 percent, and so on. Three layers of 50 percent will not reduce by the impossible amount of 150 percent but by a notional – for the figures are approximations – of 87 percent, because the second 50 percent is of 50 percent, i.e. 25 percent, and so on. This cloth is best applied outside the glass to prevent the glass getting hot. Ideally, it should be applied to a sub-frame spaced above the glass, so that its shadow falls on the glass, and air can circulate to keep the glass cool. If this is done, it is unlikely that three layers would be required very often unless you are growing orchids in conditions equivalent to the forest floor – where only a few terrestrial orchids grow.

Shade cloth is a modern equivalent of the system used up to the middle of the 20th century, when external blinds were made of laths of wood, spaced apart by links of chain, and the blind could be rolled up for storage in the winter. It is still a good system because, if the blind can be put about six inches above the roof, a pattern of ill-defined shadows moves across the plants as the sun goes across the sky, and this is very natural indeed. A project for a home-improvement enthusiast!

Internal blinds, either of simple cotton, scrim, or shade cloth, or perhaps of the latest high-tech material made for the purpose – narrow strips of aluminum foil separated by a plastic net material – are perhaps the best of all, especially if they can be motorized and linked to a mechanism. This

ABOVE a very old hybrid , but still a good one.

P. Leyburnensus "Magnificum"

enables them to be drawn back and forth under the control of some kind of sensor, so that they are extended when needed, and withdrawn when not. Of course, they do not need to be inside, although this keeps them cleaner and avoids complications with rainwater collection.

The aluminum foil blinds are the latest technology as used in the best professional orchid and plant nurseries, and are not easily available to amateur orchid growers, unless they are home-improvement enthusiasts or have extra deep pockets.

Nevertheless, high temperatures quite positively must be avoided in the orchid house by one mean or another. Thermostatically extending struts can be used to open ventilators as an alternative or additional way of providing control, and are available commercially at quite low prices. Extractor fans, operating in the same way as those used in kitchens, bathrooms, etc., and triggered by a thermostat, are another possibility.

an orchid house

ABOVE miltoniopsis, sometimes called "pansy," orchids

If you have the rare luxury of being able to build an orchid house from scratch, you should consider using a substitute for clear glass. Multi-wall polycarbonate sheet (clear, not colored) provides an insulation effect both against overheating and heat loss. It can, therefore, be simpler to keep cool, and cheaper to heat. The triple-wall version is cost efficient with insignificant light loss, and even the five-wall version, which trades even lower running costs against higher capital cost and greater light loss, might be considered.

Positive cooling devices, such as portable room air-conditioners, are a possibility. Wet-fans, or swamp coolers, where air is blown into the orchid house through a pad that is continually replenished with water, bring about quite amazing temperature reduction, although large fans may have to be ruled out as expensive to run and noisy.

It is unlikely that an orchid house can be bought, ready-made, for the trade is probably too small for there to be sufficient demand. Usually a commercially available greenhouse is converted for orchid house use, but remember that a wooden greenhouse designed as an unheated house may not be adequately treated to resist the kind of rots that can easily develop in a structure kept both warm and wet. However, a couple of coats of protective, preferably one of those containing copper salts, will deal with that. Aluminum-framed greenhouses are a possibility, but are more difficult for the orchid grower in a number of respects, and tend to seem rather colder, maybe because of heat loss through the frame, which is an excellent conductor.

There can be two different approaches to growing orchids, and maybe it is a case of does the heart dominate, or does the head. If it is the heart, the grower will fall in love with some orchids and strive to provide the conditions to grow them well. If it is the head, the grower will decide what conditions to provide, and then choose orchids that will grow in those conditions. Beware of trying to grow too many different kinds, requiring too many different conditions, all in one space. You will get the worst of all possible worlds – although many, maybe even most, beginners have been through this stage. In general, two decisions have to be made. One is whether the temperature range can be achieved. Is the cost of heating affordable? And can adequate cooling be arranged by some means? The second is whether a division can be made between bright growing orchids, and those happy with rather less light, as would be necessary if artificial light were relied upon for all the growing time.

BELOW *M. endresii* x Fred Sander

The choices then are as follows, bearing in mind that it is impossible to include 30,000 species and a hundred thousand hybrids in a short table! The temperature ranges for the various categories are given below.

cold house

Think of pleiones, and other terrestrials such as some calanthe (but caution – this is a widespread genus, and the ones from Madagascar, for example, need a warm house; you want the Asiatic ones). Also disas, those brilliantly colored large-flowered plants from the South African mountain tops, and many masdevallias.

ABOVE *Pleione* Shantung

ABOVE flowers of a terrestrial phaius species

BELOW a display of pleiones on a trade stand at an orchid show

ABOVE the disas are all summer flowering

RIGHT a first-quality modern hybrid disa. Note the width of the petals

ABOVE *Rossioglossum grande*, formerly known as *Odontoglossum grande*

LEFT *Pleione* Jorullo, typical of many stronger pink hybrids

ABOVE *Dendrobium wardianum v. lowii "Giganteum"*

cool house

Bright: Consider cymbidiums.

Less bright: Odontoglossums and soft-cane dendrobiums.

Dim: Think of other masdevallias – this genus includes many representatives suitable for any temperature regime since they are found at an enormous range of altitudes in South America – even up to 12,000 feet. Successful flowering is achieved by growing at the correct temperature for the selected plants; they will produce new leaves at the "wrong temperatures," but will not flower, or not flower well.

RIGHT *Dendrobium aureum*, also known as *D. heterocarpum*

RIGHT masdevallias, which have flower stems that are triangular in cross section ("triquetrous"), often flower for several years in succession on the same flower stems, so the old ones should not be cut off after the last flower drops. This is *M. Tovarich*.

BELOW *Odontoglossum* La Ponterrin bred by the Eric Young Foundation, home of so many magnificent hybrids

intermediate house

Bright: Cattleyas, at least those with laelia genes, miltoniopsis, and many vandas. Many dendrobiums and celogynes will also grow well, but some will need to be rested cooler in the winter in order to flower properly.

Less light: (And some would also say dim) paphs and other slippers (phrags).

LEFT an un-named hybrid using *P.* Golden Buddha as one parent

BELOW *Dendrobium kingianum*, from Australia one of the easiest to grow and flower

LEFT *Ascocenda* Fuch's Sapphire x Peggy Foo

ABOVE *Phalaenopsis stuartiana* with its distinctively marked petals

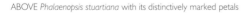

RIGHT *Vanda* Dona Roma Sanchez x *coerulea*

LEFT *Odm. pescatoreum* x *Oda* Carnetta

RIGHT *Phalaenopsis* Hausermann's Candy "York" AM/AOS

ABOVE white phalaenopsis are always stunning

BELOW *Phalaenopsis* Rose Parade x Radiant Glow

LEFT *Dendrobium* Fire Coral "Superstar"

warm house

Phalaenopsis, cattleyas (again), and vandas. Respectively these need progressively more light (phals least, vandas most). Some say that Phalaenopsis will grow in intermediate warmth, but they grow best – fastest – in warmer conditions.

Happily there are many other orchids – both species of many kinds in what may be called (without any aspersion being cast) the minor genera, and also hybrids – which will fit into any of these categories, so that any one house, even when run strictly to a particular regime, can accommodate genera by the dozen – orchids of a vast range of types and kinds in terms of flower habit, colors, and physical size, from the miniature suited to the indoor case, up to the giants needing a tall greenhouse to accommodate them.

The cold house has frost excluded. The minimum temperature will be a few degrees only above freezing, perhaps an average winter night minimum of 40 °F. Higher temperatures will occur naturally in the daytime if it is a glass structure – as is more or less implied by an assumed existence of apparatus for heating when required. Summer temperatures will be higher both by day and night, but in general very ample ventilation, and maybe shade, will keep the maximum down to 75 °F in round figures. More than this is not good for these denizens of high mountains.

The cool house will run at a winter minimum night temperature of 50 °F. It is not necessary to worry too much if the temperature drops below that occasionally, especially if the plants are dry at the time. If this is the average temperature, give or take a few degrees, all will be well for the appropriate orchids. Daytime temperatures ought to be at least 5 °F higher.

Summer temperatures should be higher by night and still higher by day, but as always, the maximum figure is just as important as the winter minimum, maybe even more so, and sometimes difficult to keep below – 75 °F would be wonderful. More would be acceptable, especially if only occasionally and not regularly, but over 90 °F is undesirable and could well be fatal for some odonts. Over 100 degrees F is a recipe for cooking an early death for any orchid.

BELOW once known as *Odontoglossum nebulosum*, and now agreed to belong elsewhere – but botanists do not agree where

When an intermediate house is considered, the figures all take another 5 °F lift, as far as minimums are concerned, but the summer maximums are not increased.

The same applies to the hot house – a winter night temperature of 65 °F is essential, and a summer night temperature could be 70 °F minimum. However, the maximum at any time of day should not be more than the odd degree or so over the 90 °F mark.

A greenhouse becomes an orchid house when it is converted to provide what orchids need. Much of this is a matter of heating, shading, ventilation, humidification systems, and the like, but benches should not be overlooked. They need to be robust because a collection of pots can be quite heavy, particularly when some older plants are in the large sizes of pots. Again, you can build your own, although ready-made benches in slatted aluminum are available in a range of widths, lengths, and heights, usually flat-packed for easy home assembly, and often with the possibility of providing a shelf just below the bench level for wet gravel to aid humidification – the so called wet-bench system.

RIGHT *Odontoglossum crispum*, line-bred through many generations of what have been called hybrids, to be far superior to the original species

ABOVE *Odm. cervantesii*

watering

ABOVE a miniature-flowered ascocenda – the flowers are about an inch across

BELOW bulbophyllum is a very large genus and one of the few with a circumpolar distribution.

Bulbophyllum graveolens

This is probably the most important subject in orchid growing. Beginners may be forgiven for being puzzled when everyone tells them so, but then no one ever tells them how often a plant should be watered. This is because the question is almost comparable to "how long is a piece of string?" The answer to both being, "it all depends."

It has often been said that overwatering kills more orchids than any other cause. Overwatering will, or can, waterlog the plant, and then the roots die. Orchids are tough, long-suffering, and great survivors but, eventually, a plant with no roots has to die. However, this does not mean that water should be dribbled into a plant pot at long intervals – for the other main cause of orchid death is underwatering. When the plant becomes desiccated, the roots shrivel, and once again the plant dies.

Let us start with the action of watering. It is impossible to give a plant too much water on any one occasion. Don't dribble. Soak. Overwatering does not mean giving too much each time you water, it means watering at too frequent intervals.

When the plant has been soaked, lift it up and watch the water pour out of the pot. This indicates the drainage is good, and that is almost the first essential for any orchid. If it only dribbles out, then the drainage is bad, and has to be improved – fast (see pages 98 onwards).

There is one safe rule about the interval before the next watering. After the plant has been given this good soak, and has drained, it will do no harm at all to wait until the plant is beginning to get dry before it is watered again. Better than 99.99 percent of all orchids love to alternate between wet and dry, and are adapted to do just that. However, in the wild, they may be soaked at dawn, and dry by midday, and that is very hard to replicate in cultivation.

When an orchid is in its most vigorous growth phase it can tolerate an almost unbelievable amount of water, and even experienced cultivators may be giving less than the plant would actually like. And when an orchid is in the no-growth phase, maybe after flowering and before starting a new growth, the converse applies. And again, even experienced growers may be giving more than the plant really wants. It is only because orchids are so tough and long-suffering that it is possible not only to grow them, but also to do very well with them, despite not giving them exactly what they would like. In support of these statements, consider a plant in

ABOVE *Bonatea speciosa*, a South African terrestrial needing a cold and dry winter rest

the wild, say in a forest where the rainfall is measured not in inches but in yards. Many Central American forests on the Caribbean side have well over 200 inches of rain in a year, most of which falls in about eight months of the year. It may not rain every day, although sometimes it does, but that averages out to six inches of rain a week. And in the "dry" season it may not rain heavily for months, although in some areas mists, fogs, and dew will refresh the plants every night.

If the safe method of watering when nearly dry is followed, the next question is how to tell. Many experts advise lifting the pot, and gauging the weight. This may work very well for the expert – maybe a professional – in a nursery with a batch of a hundred identical pots of the same plant – when variations will be easy to sense. But it is useless for the hobbyist whose every pot is a different size and contains a different kind of plant. Of course the cymbidium in a 10-inch pot is heavy (wet or dry) and the seedling in a 2-inch pot is light (wet or dry). Looking at the top of the compost is not much help because some composts dry out very quickly on the surface and remain sodden below.

There is a foolproof way, however, based on weight, which is to use kitchen scales. The kind with a digital display in grams is excellent since 5 grams is 1 teaspoonful of water, and 600 grams is 1 pint of water – both of which are easy to visualize. Weigh the plant soon after it has been watered, when it is well drained, but before it starts to dry – an hour after the watering. Note the weight and pencil it on the label. When you think that it needs watering, weigh it again, and a subtraction exercise will show how much water has been lost. Of the total weight, some is due to the pot – not much if it is a plastic pot, but quite a lot if a clay pot is used. Not much is due to the plant itself, unless it is a cymbidium with a lot of big bulbs. Most is due to the compost and water. As the most extreme generalization, plants need watering when 10–20 percent of the weight has been lost since the last watering. It is possible to get this down to a much more accurate figure by doing a first weighing after the plant has been repotted, and before the first watering. The second weighing of the wet plant will reveal the total water retained in the pot. Usually not more than half of that should be used before re-watering, for some of it tends to be locked up in the compost and so not readily available.

When you have grown a plant successfully for a time, you will gain experience, and the whole watering process becomes simpler. But do remember that summer means longer days and higher temperatures, plants

ABOVE standard – large-flowered – cymbidiums can have quite big bulbs, the size of a large potato for example. This one is C. Mavourneen "Jester"

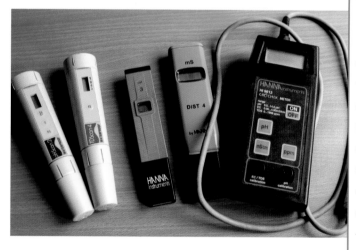

ABOVE a selection of testing meters including a combination pH and conductivity meter with a probe on a wander lead

will transpire more water, and thus need watering more frequently, even if not in an active growth phase – and of course vice versa.

One indication to look out for is new roots. Watering should be minimal at this time to encourage those roots to grow and search for water, and in so doing (hopefully) fill the pot. But it is a sign that maximum watering will very soon be needed. Work up to it as the roots extend, and certainly reach maximum when the new growth can be seen to be rapidly enlarging.

The very best water for orchids is clean rain. If collected, it should, ideally, come from a glass, plastic, or slate roof – or from any other material where there is no chance of contamination creeping into the water. Cement tiles, especially after a longish dry spell, can give up tiny particles of cement – old roofs wear thin because the cement washes into the rainwater – and a tiny amount of cement is very alkaline and makes the water unsuitable for orchids. However, if there is a rainy spell, although the first rainfall should be discarded, it will likely have washed away all the particles loose at one time, and the next lot of rain may well be safe and usable. If in doubt, test the pH – the measure of acidity/alkalinity.

The pH testing can be done with test papers, or with a product where a few drops of the water and product are mixed and the color compared on a chart, or with a meter. The enthusiast with a collection of orchids will want the meter, typically costing less than $50.

The ideal pH figure for orchids, by general agreement, is between about pH 5.7 and 6.2. Remember that pH 7.0 is 10 times as alkaline as 6.0, pH 8 is 100 times as alkaline as 6.0, and so on. For alkalinity, read as for acidity, but going in the opposite direction.

Acidity and alkalinity can be adjusted with products that are often available from aquarium and fish-keepers suppliers under names such as pH "up" and pH "down". These are potent chemicals and are best used very well diluted. Wear old clothes, a face mask (available from agricultural suppliers), and rubber gloves. Kitchen gloves are fine. Take a plastic bottle, such as an empty drinks container, remove the label, fill the bottle to within an inch of the top with water (tap water is fine), and add the chemical to fill it. This will be a reasonable dilution for use, but even then only a few drops will be needed in a large bucket of water to make an adjustment of maybe 0.5 pH. And do store the product and diluted product in a safe place out of the reach of children.

For small collections, vinegar or lemon juice can be used to acidify (reduce the pH) and ammonia to alkanize (raise the pH).

Testing and adjustment, at least for nutrient content rather than acidity, is likely to be much more necessary if you do not use rainwater. Tap water varies very considerably, depending on where it comes from. Deep bore water from intensely cultivated areas may well have a lot of agricultural fertilizer in it. In other areas, where

ABOVE a small RO kit. The red pipe is mains water in, the black is pure water out, and the blue is waste (for orchids) water

scale develops in kettles, there may be a lot of lime in it. Rain, of course, has virtually nothing in it, apart from gases picked up in its fall through the atmosphere. However, in dirty industrial areas with polluting chimneys, it could be so bad as to be unusable.

Very pure, or fairly pure water may be produced using reverse osmosis (RO) equipment, which effectively filters the water. This works on high pressure and low volume flow, but the portion containing the separated chemicals from the water may be four or five times the volume of the purer water. In other words, each gallon of water for the orchids may lead to five gallons of unsuitable water, which could be used up on ordinary garden plants or for other purposes; a consideration to be borne in mind if you are paying for the amount of water used.

Of course, any water is better than no water at all. If you have been using rain, but then there is dry spell, you must use water from faucets, or some other source.

nutrients

All green plants need nutrients. The major ones are usually marked on the fertilizer package as N.P.K. Although agricultural chemists will be horrified at an over-simplification, very broadly speaking the N (nitrogen) is needed for the green parts of the plant, the P (phosphorus) for the flowers, and the K (potash) for the roots. A good many other things are needed, some in relatively large amounts, some in smaller amounts, and some in incredibly minute amounts. However, if a plant needs one atom of boron for every so many million atoms of nitrogen, it will be an imperfect plant without that one atom.

Two of the other nutrients that sometimes give difficulty are calcium – needed to make the wall of every cell of the plant – and magnesium. There is a single atom of magnesium at the center of each molecule of chlorophyll, which is the powerhouse of the plant, turning water and air into plant sugars. And the difficulty is that if both are included in the fertilizer there may be problems with solubility, that is, the fertilizer may not dissolve well in water, and there may be precipitation, meaning that each plant does not get its intended share of both of these elements. There is a way round this, however, as described on page 93.

ABOVE coconut-fiber chunks

Research supports the view that it is best to provide fertilizer at every watering, in a weak solution, rather than more heavily at longer intervals. How much to provide is a controversial question, because it depends on other factors, such as the nature of the compost, whether the plant is growing or at rest, and the amount of light provided. If an inorganic compost, which means a mineral one (rockwool, perlite, etc.), is used, there may be no nutrient in the material apart from what is added in the water. If bark, peat, or any other organic material is used, there is some feed provided by the compost, and it could be that less nutrient needs to be added.

But alas, the question is not quite that simple. What is added in the water is not necessarily available to the plant. The compost inevitably contains bacteria – present in soil, and likely to have been introduced on the roots of the plant. The bacteria break down the nutrients, however provided, incidentally making them available to the plant, but taking a disproportionate share of certain of the nutrients for themselves. If bark is in the compost, extra nitrogen has to be added to allow for this.

If tap water is used, it already contains some chemicals, and if these are the kinds that make for hard water, white powdery deposits may be left on the leaves. This is unsightly, but that is by no means the worst of it. Water suppliers publish, or will usually make available, a typical analysis. Some of what is there may be usable by the orchid. Some is not. This is because part may be in a salt form, which the plant cannot handle, or maybe because it is something the plant wants in

ABOVE the summer-flowering *Thunia gattonensis*, which rests dry and cold in the winter

barely measurable quantities, such as silica or aluminum, but which is present in the water in rather greater quantities.

What is in the water, wanted or not, has an effect. And part of that effect is that if fertilizer is added in quite modest quantities to water that already has a charge of chemicals, a surprisingly strong solution can be produced. "Strong" chemical solutions can scorch roots and damage orchids. The kind of concentration that is strong for an orchid would not be strong for most garden plants. However, it may be present in water out of the faucet with nothing added to it. (Such water may be perfectly good and palatable for humans.)

All of the above explains why rain and RO water are the preferred choices. If there is nothing already in the water, or very little, the grower can add what the orchid wants, as well as adding it in the correct proportions. But do not let all this talk deter you. Why not try tap water with your first plant – assuming you do not have rainwater readily available – and see how it does. Very many orchid growers use nothing else.

If an actual orchid fertilizer is used, do read the label very carefully. Does the manufacturer make any assumption as to the nature of the water? If the label says rain, and this is what is being used, then the label can be followed as to strength. In almost any other case, it may be safer to use a much, much weaker concentration. The same applies if using a general garden fertilizer bought from a garden center – use at only a quarter of the suggested strength.

If the tap water proves to be unusable – plants rapidly sicken with it – and the collection is to consist of a very few plants, the expense of RO will not be justifiable, and if there is no rain, what can be done? There are other sources of pure water – ask for de-ionized water at the drug store, or distilled water. Some electrical appliances handling water, such as tumble dryers, have built-in condensers, and fill a tank with the condensate. This is quite chemically pure (even if

not biologically pure) and can be used safely. The same applies to dehumidifiers and portable air-conditioners.

The "strength" of water, or a water/fertilizer solution can be measured. The grower with more than a few plants will be well advised to make an investment in the appropriate kit – again it is a pocket-size meter available at a cost of $50, or thereabouts, depending on the make, model, and sophistication. What is measured here is the conductivity of the solution, which is nowadays measured in Siemens, or some fraction of this. Avoid TDS (total dissolved salt) meters, which only give approximations of content. There is controversy about precise levels, but the majority of experienced growers will probably agree that, for phalaenopsis, a figure of 750 microSiemens is maximal, that cymbidiums will accept almost as much as 600, and that paphiopedilums prefer lower levels such as 500 mS maximum. Disas, on the other hand, grow on the edges of streams, where occasionally the water level rises and may even submerge them. The stream water reads about 200 mS, indicating much lower levels for these orchids. They can possibly be given 300mS as a maximum, but not often.

Tap water may be as low as 250mS in "good" areas, and as high as 900 in bad ones. This explains why most growers using tap water manage to kill disas in a season – even if they never add any fertilizer – and why phalaenopsis are the easiest orchids.

Consequently, it may be said that, if using a meter and adjusting the water/fertilizer concentration, a figure of about 400–500 mS is suitable for most orchids, except disas. Even the ones that "will take" 750 mS, grow very well – hardly distinguishably different – at 400 mS.

compost

If organic compost is employed – bark or coconut-fiber chunks, the fertilizer speeds the breakdown of these materials. Of course it is in the breakdown that nutrients are released from the bark, but the higher the concentration, the more frequently repotting will be needed.

As implied earlier, most fertilizers made for garden use do not contain any, or at least enough, calcium and magnesium, because sufficient is available in the soil, or in tap water (fertilizer manufacturers making for yard or garden usage assume that tap water will be mixed with their product). Both of these can be added separately to the mix made up by the orchid grower – but not together, because that would likely cause one to precipitate out – or better still used separately and periodically as foliar feeding by spraying.

The calcium can be added in the form of calcium nitrate – sometimes available from garden centers, or if not, from specialty garden suppliers. Mix 3oz. in just under a quart – but the precise amount of weight or water is not too significant – to make a stock solution, which should be kept out of bright light. This can be added to water at the rate of a teaspoonful of stock per gallon of water for use on its own, that is, for watering plants. Or it can be mixed into the general fertilizer/water mix at the same rate, using the meter to adjust to the desired level. Or, it can be sprayed at the rate of a tablespoon per gallon. It helps to add a drop of wetting agent, such as a detergent or dish-washing liquid to the sprayer.

Similarly, Epsom salts, obtained from a drug

ABOVE fine bark

store, has the chemical formula $MgSO_4$ or magnesium sulfate. This can be treated precisely in the same way as calcium nitrate except that it is unnecessary to make up a stock solution, and the salts can be added to the water in the same proportions – a teaspoon of salts per gallon for watering, or a tablespoon of salts per gallon, plus wetting agent, for foliar feeding.

Both of the foliar feeding programs can be followed, alternately, at monthly intervals – spray with calcium one month, and magnesium the next month.

A great number of different composts or soils have been used for growing orchids, at one time or another, and very good results have been achieved with very many of them. This goes to show how adaptable orchids are, considering that in the wild very few orchids actually grow in any kind of soil or compost at all! Also, compost is expensive to ship around the world, meaning that any grower has to find something available locally. This has led to experiments with many exotic materials – for example, in the Canary Islands a mixture of sawdust and volcanic ash is used successfully.

However, the two most popular materials today for hobbyists and professionals alike are bark mixes and rockwool. Bark is tree bark. Not bark from any old tree, but usually bark from a conifer or fir tree. Pine bark is popular in North America, and redwood bark is also used there. In Europe it is often fir bark, most frequently Douglas fir. This bark may come in pieces about the size of a grain of rice (seedling bark intended for growing tiny plants), or rather larger flakes the size of a fingernail but thicker, up to chunks larger than a sugar cube or unshelled walnut. The larger pieces are used for thicker rooted plants – vandas, cattleyas and the smaller pieces for the finer rooted-genera.

ABOVE different grades of bark and perlite

bark

Bark is usually mixed with other ingredients, notably perlite and charcoal. Perlite "opens" the compost, makes it drain better, and contributes to a mix that can be poured, rather than placed, into a pot. Charcoal sweetens the mix, which means (in theory) that it keeps the mix good for longer. Bark is one of the best possible composts for most orchids, and is obviously very natural for plants that commonly grow on trees, despite the fact that orchids do not grow on fir trees, which come from temperate climates. But, beware – bark breaks down as it is watered, and this changes its nature. At a certain point bark starts to break down very rapidly and then becomes over acid. It then makes very bad compost for orchids. Orchids in bark must be repotted regularly before this breakdown happens. Plants in small pots, up to about 3½ inches diameter, need watering frequently and consequently need repotting frequently. Once every six months is not too often for plants in thumb pots up to 2 ½ inches in diameter. Plants in larger pots – 6 inches diameter or above – need watering less frequently and can go 12 months or longer between repotting. Plants in very large pots, especially if rested quite dry for several months of the year, can go even longer. Sometimes very large, old, well-established plants, called "specimen" plants, may simply be top-dressed with fresh compost each year. They will go on for many years before eventually they are split up, and repotted in fresh compost, to start all over again. If repotting is not carried out when it is needed, the acidity will kill the roots and the plant will suffer a severe setback. Once this has happened the damage is done, even if the plant is repotted, and it may take a few years before the plant is restored to full vigor.

A typical bark mix is 1 part each of perlite and charcoal to 4 parts bark. Mixes like this can be purchased from orchid specialty nurseries that use it themselves.

rockwool

The second main material used today is rockwool. This is indeed made from a mineral (rock) material. It may look like rather dirty (gray) absorbent cotton, although another brand is golden yellow. There are two kinds, one of which absorbs (holds) water, while the other repels (does not hold) water. The two are mixed according to the grower's fancy. Usually ready-made mixtures are 2 parts of absorbent to 1 part of repellent, sometimes with perlite added in 1 part to 2 or 3 or 4 of rockwool. Rockwool does not breakdown or rot, and in theory this makes it last for ever. In practice, it is usually desirable to replace it periodically because of an unavoidable buildup of salts in the pots from unused fertilizer, etc., In addition, it seems that rockwool's natural neutrality changes over time and it becomes too alkaline, maybe due to a component slowly leaching out.

Rockwool has one peculiarity. The fibers can be a skin irritant, and continued exposure to them can cause skin problems. It is not so dangerous that it must never be touched, unless the user has become sensitized to it, but it is at least very desirable to wear rubber gloves when handling it. Some hobbyists apply skin cream and don rubber gloves for all greenhouse and growing operations – it keeps dirt out of fingernails, and for the squeamish it may be easier (and is certainly more hygienic) to squash any discovered nasty creepy crawler when wearing them!

Remember that rockwool is usually kept much wetter than bark, and that a plant grown in it will need watering perhaps three times as often as a plant in bark. Overwatering rockwool carries much less risk than it would to a plant in bark. Rockwool itself contains no nutrients (Greenmix by Grodan is an exception). If the container makes no mention of added nutrients, it should be assumed that everything has to be added. Bark, on the other hand, is easier to use without risk of inflicting physical damage to the roots during the repotting operation (see page 98).

ABOVE dried sterile sphagnum moss, after soaking and draining

other materials

Other materials that you may encounter include coconut husk chunks (or chips). This is a newish material for the purpose, although in areas where coconuts are grown it has long been used for orchids. In those places they take the coconut whole, cut off one end, make a slit in the soft and springy center, and place the plant in that slit. This is very good for dendrobiums in particular.

Coconut husk chunk advocates say it is better than bark. It can hold more water – allowing longer intervals between watering – and paradoxically also hold more air, giving good rooting results. It is also said to last at least twice as long before repotting is needed. Its disadvantage is that it needs to be washed extremely thoroughly with several complete changes of water to remove unwanted salts (often including sea salt) before it is safe to use.

Peat was for many years a favorite material, but the world's supply has diminished and it is unlikely to reappear as a readily available material that the conservation-conscious grower will want to use. On the other hand, sphagnum moss (one of the ingredients of peat) seems to grow in large quantities in several countries, and it seems likely that harvesting is either sustainable, or desirable in the interests of land improvement. The hobbyist may buy sterile dried imported New Zealand or Chilean moss with a clear conscience. It is readied for use simply by breaking down the mini-bale and soaking in water. It makes good compost on its own, especially for fine-rooted, bulbless plants such as masdevallias and pleurothallids and a good "recovery" compost for rootless orchids of all kinds.

ABOVE *Phaius tankervillae*, to be seen in most tropical countries, sometimes native and often introduced

In the not too distant past, osmunda fiber was used, usually mixed with sphagnum moss. Osmunda is a fern, and the fiber was the dead root mass. This mixture grew good orchids, although its use needed developed skills, but it went out of favor because the world supply was inadequate and prices rocketed. It is still occasionally seen, but little used since, arguably, far better results can be achieved with other materials. Tree fern fiber is often used in blocks for growing orchids out of pots – simply tied to the block – and occasionally as a mix ingredient.

And finally cork, which is of course the bark of an oak tree, is widely used both in large pieces as a mount or plaque for suitable orchids (out of pot) and in chip-sized pieces as a compost ingredient. Some wine buffs save their corks, use them as a compost material, suitably broken up into rough chunks, and swear that the traces of wine left on the corks provide valuable nutrition. However, the cork does not easily wet, and more frequent watering may be needed.

Terrestrial orchids need rather more water-retentive compost. Those from the woodlands, where the soil is enriched with annual leaf fall, such as calanthe and phaius, will need a rich mixture. This tends to mean one made from organic materials (bark rather than rockwool), with additions of leaf mold, loam fiber, coconut fiber, or the like. Leaf mold is best made from oak or beech leaves, collected in the fall, placed in a plastic bag with a few holes to let the air in and out, and hung up in a garage or cellar for a year or two, then rubbed through a sieve to make a crumbly, dark, dry mixture. Loam fiber is made by stacking grass turfs upside down for a year to kill the roots, then shaking them through a coarse sieve to remove most of the soil.

Other terrestrials come from poor low-nutrient gravels, and many of the African species – spathoglottis, disas and other wetland types, bonatea, and some habenaria, for example – will need a lean mixture made of gravel, grit, coarse sand, and just a trace of peat or leaf mold. Almost every experienced grower has his or her own recipe for these mixtures, which may mean that the exact composition is not critical. But, as always, for both rich and lean mixtures, the mix must drain quickly even if it does end up holding moisture. If there is any doubt, then add extra perlite or grit to improve drainage.

Another compost material popular with many growers is furniture upholstery foam, in small pieces about the same size as orchid bark. This is often mixed with rockwool, using only the water-absorbent kind, for the foam is water repellent. The mix is springy and squashy, which means that it can help grip the plant firmly in position. Only gentle finger pressure is needed to push the mixture into the pot.

repotting

This is needed from time to time for any of a number of reasons. One is that the plant has outgrown the pot, which will be self-evident. Another is that the compost needs to be replaced. This is more difficult for the tyro hobbyist to detect. For anyone who has invested in the two meters mentioned in connection with water and fertilizers, there is an easy solution to the problem.

Flood a pot with pure water, drain it, collect the last of the drainings, and take readings of pH and EC (electrical conductivity). If you use rainwater, or similarly very pure water, it will have had an EC of 20 mS, or even lower. The pH may have been anywhere between 5 and 7. Now see what the figures are for the last drainings from the pot. Suppose the pH is now

4. This kind of figure is produced by bark composts going sour and shows that the compost must be particularly acid – too acid for the good of the plant. It is likely in this situation that the EC will also be much higher than that of the water that went in, again indicating either that the compost has become saturated with high concentration fertilizer, or that it is breaking down and releasing salts into the water. In either case, early repotting is required. Frequent flushing with pure water and/or top-dressing the compost with a teaspoonful of dolomitic lime (containing both calcium and magnesium) is an interim measure and may save the plant. If rockwool is the material, then old compost may have a much higher pH – maybe 8.0 – again indicating a need for immediate action. Finally, repotting will be needed if the drainage is suspect. If, after flooding the pot, the water does not drain out rapidly, the compost may have broken down and filled the drainage holes with mud.

If you do not have meters to make tests, you should repot annually if using organic mixes (bark), and biannually if using inorganic mixes, as a safety precaution.

practical requirements

There are three important requirements to be met in potting. First, at the end of the operation, the plant must be secure and not shaky in the pot. If not secure, the new roots will bruise every time the plant wobbles, for the precious green (usually) growing tip is very sensitive and easily damaged. If a plant does wobble, it must be secured. One way of doing this is a simple stake and tie. If necessary, canes can be wired to the pot so that they are secure, and then the plant tied to the canes. Second, the drainage must be perfect at the end of the potting operation. If not, you will have to start again, taking care to find out why the drainage was imperfect. Does the pot need larger drainage holes? Was the compost too powdery so that it compacted?

Third, potting should be accomplished without ramming or pushing the compost into place, as this will damage the roots. "Pourable" compost makes this operation easy. But if the chosen compost is not one that can be poured, extra care has to be taken. If you use sphagnum moss, the plant roots can be gently wrapped into a ball surrounded by new moss. Place the ball in a pot, and push in sufficient extra moss, very gently, until the plant is firm and secure.

It is easier to avoid damage to roots if new roots have not yet started to grow. This means that the potting operation should be timed – assuming it is not being done as an emergency treatment but as a routine – to take place when new growths have initiated but are only a few inches high. Most orchids produce a new set of roots from new growths at this kind of height, and if they can go straight into new compost, so much the better.

BELOW an odontoglossum plant being repotted. Note the good
root structure which should be disturbed as little as possible

Repotting consists of knocking the plant out of its old pot, shaking off as much as possible of the old compost, tidying the plant up by removing unwanted old growths and leafless back bulbs, trimming off dead roots using sharp scissors sterilized in alcohol, holding the plant in a clean new pot of the right size, and then pouring in the new compost. What is the right size? One that allows the whole root ball to be accommodated without cramping the roots, and no larger, and that has sufficient space to accommodate the plant until the next expected repotting.

The plant should be positioned in the pot at an appropriate height, so that the growths emerge from the compost half an inch, or thereabouts, below the rim of the pot, to allow for watering. Fine-rooted plants should be placed so that most of the roots will be covered by compost. It is particularly desirable with these to watch the level very carefully. If the new roots emerge above the compost they are easily damaged by pill bugs (also known as woodlice), but are safe from them if they emerge below the level of the compost.

It is necessary to emphasize that if you are not using pourable compost, it is important to avoid ramming. Sphagnum moss, for example, if used on its own, can be quite loose and will still hold a plant firmly. If rammed in, apart from the risk of damaging roots, it can also drain poorly and give bad growing conditions. Rockwool can be placed in a pot a pinch at a time, or if used for large pots – such as those needed for cymbidiums that are to be grown on into large plants – a handful at a time. Do not forget to put a new label in with the repotted plant.

Old used pots are perfectly reusable, after cleaning. Drop used pots into a bucket of water, containing a good dash of household bleach, and leave them to soak. After a day or so, most dirt wipes off.

Beginners are often told to repot in the spring or fall. These are the best times, but if a plant is found to need repotting it is better to do it whatever the day of the year.

LEFT new shoots and new roots just emerging, ideally the
plant should have been repotted two weeks earlier

plaque mounts and baskets

ABOVE a plaque mount

Plants that grow wild on the more vertical parts of trees, rather than on horizontal branches, often do well on plaque mounts, rather than in pots. Plaques are often pieces of cork bark. The plants are held in place by a discreet and near invisible length of nylon fishing line, until such time as new roots wander over the cork to grip and hold the plant in place. A few plants on plaques, hanging up in the orchid room, give an exotic air to a collection, especially if the plants treated this way have pendant (directed downward) flower spikes. But they do need regular attention, preferably misting with water at least once a day, if they are to do well.

A plaque is usually a vertical surface. Plants that like to be dry between watering also do well on rafts, which are much the same thing, but arranged horizontally rather than vertically.

Rafts and plaques are usually hung up near the roof of the orchid room. This means that they will be in a warmer and brighter environment than plants in pots on a bench or table below. Warm air rises! This can be an advantage if you are growing a plant that needs slightly different conditions than the rest of the collection.

baskets

Basket culture is another possibility. Traditional orchid baskets are made from slats of wood, usually teak. They are almost essential for some orchids that live in the wild on horizontal branches and send their flower spikes straight down, but are unhappy on rafts, because they need a greater depth of compost (in fact, it is difficult to provide any compost on a raft). If such orchids are grown in a pot, the flower spike disappears into the compost and is never seen. Stanhopeas, gongoras, some coelogynes, and papaphinia are some of the orchids with bulbs that fall into this category. Draculas – those fascinating close relatives of masdevallia – are an example among the bulbless orchids.

However, many modern composts pose something of a problem in baskets. Osmunda fiber and moss mixtures make the ideal compost mixture. Bark mixtures are not contained between the slats of a basket too well, and rockwool dries out too quickly in the airy situation of a basket. The modern equivalent, while not as aesthetically appealing as a teak basket, is a square of wire mesh, especially the plastic-coated kind, cut with scissors, and bent into the desired shape. You can make it to the desired size too, instead of having to settle for the nearest size available in a wooden basket. By finding a suitable mesh size, almost any compost can be accommodated.

There is one instance where wooden baskets are still used widely, without any compost at all, and that is with vandas and their relatives grown in the Far East. When first seen, the beginner may think that something is missing – just an empty basket with a plant standing up in it.

BELOW a terete-leaved vanda – the leaves are like knitting needles – a natural adaption against high light and limiting the transpiration rate of the plant

However, the roots grow along the wood and hold the plant in place, and then more roots hang out into the air. Of course the absence of compost means that very regular soaking with sprays is needful – twice a day in the growing season and maybe every few days in a resting season so as to soak the roots. In Thailand they have great success with this system, but growers in cooler countries often report that growth rates slacken off after a season or so, and it is necessary to transfer the plants to more conventional pots in order to keep them growing and flowering.

RIGHT a pendant-flowered cymbidium growing in a basket

BELOW vandas in plastic baskets, which are beginning to replace the traditional wooden ones

hydroponics

This word means "growing without soil." Some hobbyists who use this system also use, and indeed prefer, the word "hydroculture," which means growing in water. There are two methods.

BELOW *Phragmepedium sedenii* – a slipper orchid making large plants which flower for six months on end.

method 1

In the first, the plants are placed in pots containing some kind of coarse granular mineral material, which is not water soluble, as a compost. In some places small pebbles are used as the mineral, and in others well-washed coarse volcanic ash. Two suitable materials seem to be available worldwide from garden centers, namely perlite and manufactured clay pebbles, often sold under trade names such as Hortag, Perlag, Hydroleca. These pebbles are a rusty brown color, smooth, and like irregular ball bearings, usually (and desirably) about $\frac{1}{4}$ –$\frac{1}{2}$-inch diameter. The plant is

positioned at a suitable height in the pot, the mineral is poured in, and that is it. However, it is also possible to top-dress the surface of the compost, as a final ½ inch of the compost, with a grit – ordinary horticultural grit from a garden center or indoor fish-keepers supply store – so as to provide a better grip to hold a wobbly plant in place, and also in situations where root nibbling pests are a nuisance, to hide the delicate root tips.

If using a smaller grained material such as perlite, which even in the coarse grade is typically of less than ¼ inch size (and may well be only half that), it is useful to carefully lower the pot into a bucket of water, as far as the rim, and then after a rapid draining gently tap the pot on a hard surface to settle the grains around the roots.

The pot is then stood in a saucer, or if there are several, the pots are stood in a dish or tray or even – when "several" means a lot – a shallow tank, containing water and nutrient mix, with a depth of water of typically rather less than one inch. And that's it!

The water will be carried up the granular material in each pot by capillary action. If you are unfamiliar with this, try placing a sugar cube on a spoon containing just a little coffee and see how the coffee moves up through the cube. This is capillary action. The water evaporates at the top of the pot, so that the top is driest, and the foot of the pot in the water is wettest. Roots, at least orchid roots, will die if permanently in water, so those below water level will rot. But new roots will find their own level where the moisture is just what they like.

The saucer will need to be filled up with more water, but without extra nutrients. This is because it is mostly water that evaporates at the top; the nutrients stay behind in the pot. If it is a larger vessel, it will need to be emptied and refilled with correct nutrient solution periodically, meaning perhaps once a month.

This system suits many orchids that are in perpetual growth, such as odonts and hard-caned dendrobiums. Moreover, they can grow and flower much better than is usually possible in a regime where they are watered at only intervals of days or weeks. For orchids that want a rest, the system can be used for the growing season. Resting can then be carried out either dry, or using water without nutrient addition, especially when a temperature drop is arranged – a bedroom with heating turned off perhaps for those growing indoors, or a separate and less heated greenhouse for those in cooler climes growing outdoors.

flood and drain

There is a second system, known as "flood and drain," which requires some kind of automated plumbing system, and is therefore more appropriate for a larger collection. A deeper tank is used so that it can be flooded to a depth just less than the pot rim level. The tank is held at that level for a few minutes and then drained. It is easy to set up simple timers and appropriate control valves, for example, those used for central heating water flow, to construct a setup which, when running satisfactorily, can be safely left for weeks at a time in the secure knowledge that the plants are being watered every day at noon, or whatever.

Frequency of flooding depends on so many factors. Using the largest clay pebbles and growing vandas and cattleyas, three floods per day in midsummer, reducing to one every few days in midwinter, give good results. And incidentally, drying out for a week or two does not seem to matter too much with plants that have been grown well and are full and turgid, so that an occasional failure with a home-made rig-up is not too disastrous.

If nutrition is strictly controlled by using conductivity meters (see page 88), levels can, apparently, be much higher with hydroponic systems than in more conventional culture. This is possibly because strong plants growing fast can take more food, or maybe it is because of the low carry-up of the salts in the capillary action. Whatever the reason, the levels can be increased by at least 50 percent.

Hydroponics/hydroculture is controversial, and not many hobbyists and very few professionals use it. However, the great reduction in work time – the chores of orchid growing – which it can provide, and the remarkable results that a few users are obtaining and publicizing, mean that it could well be the way of the future.

propagation

Of course, early European orchid growers would have tried to sow seed, but with very little success. Successful seed raising is very difficult with orchids for reasons which were not understood at all for a very long time. Orchids are absolutely prodigal in the vast amount of seed produced, with many species producing seedpods containing seeds numbered in hundreds of thousands. Since the world is not entirely covered knee-deep in orchids it is obvious that very few actually germinate and grow. With perseverance, skilled gardeners discovered that, by sowing the seed around the mother plant, a few seedlings would germinate. It seemed that the compost around the mother contained something that the seeds needed to start out in life.

By the second half of the 19th century there were more than a few growers sufficiently skilled to be successful in raising new plants, but only in small numbers, so that it was not – and never did become – a commercial proposition. While this was true, any demand for orchids could only be met by collecting from the jungle. Given the difficulties and risks this involved in the days before vaccinations and air travel, it is not surprising that the plants that reached the auction rooms fetched remarkable prices.

At some point in the history of seed raising growers discovered symbiosis and realized why so few seedlings were produced from so much

BELOW slipper orchids give relatively few seeds, and some hybrids are so highly bred as to be near-sterile and give none. The picutre shows the species *P. villosum*

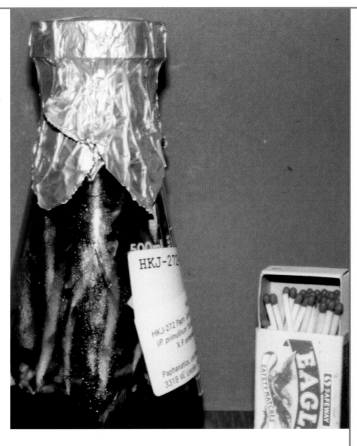

ABOVE a flask of orchid seedlings – with a box of matches to give scale

seed. Almost every orchid species is capable of entering into a symbiotic relationship with a particular – and perhaps different – microfungus. Usually, when not involved with orchid seed, the fungus has the role of digesting necrotic vegetable tissue and effectively recycling the component chemicals. However, when the hyphae (extending filaments) of the fungus invade the germinating orchid seed there is some kind of mutual exchange, so that the seed receives minerals which, at least at that stage, it is not able to obtain for itself, and maybe the fungus obtains sugars from the photosynthesis beginning to be carried out by the developing seed. At all events, the seed is not destroyed – or at least, maybe some or even many are destroyed, but some survive and flourish and grow to become plants. When those early hybridists succeeded with their seeds sown around the mother plant

the necessary microfungus would have been associated with it in the compost, no doubt imported from its original jungle setting on the roots of the collected plant.

In the first quarter of the 20th century, when the symbiotic relationship had been worked out, other workers discovered what the microfungus was supplying and devised formulae to supply the same. This meant that seeds could be sown assymbiotically on sterile agar jelly impregnated with the required nutrients in the right balance. From that time onward, it was possible (in ideal cases) to germinate the vast majority of seeds. This enabled the mass production of orchids.

For very many years this system was used to raise new orchid hybrids – crosses between different species – but hardly ever to raise species. There was no need because the jungles were full of species and it was cheaper to collect rather than raise them. And while modern conservationists will shake their heads ruefully at this acquiescence in jungle stripping, the fact is also that once hybrids were raised, they were generally found to be much easier to grow. In addition, nursery-raised plants that have not been dehydrated and sent half around the world in darkness are likely to be better plants anyway. As a result, growers wanted hybrids, and species took a back seat. Collecting diminished, and the days of fortunes being paid at the auction rooms for a new species ended forever.

All of this may give the impression that, now the secret is known, orchid seed raising is easy. Certainly it is easy enough for a good many serious hobbyists to practice it on the kitchen table, but a brief explanation of what is involved will show that a lot of skill and expertise is involved.

First, the seedpods need to be at an appropriate stage of ripeness, which may take anything from a month to a year, depending on the orchid and the way it has been grown. If the pod is too ripe it will split (dehisce), allowing the dustlike seed to drift out into the air and spread. However, that also allows contamination of the seed, which almost destroys any chance of it being raised successfully. Contamination comes from spores floating in the air – the same spores that will lead to mold on jam or cheese. Sterilization is possible, but with such a minute fragile thing as a dustlike seed, a chlorox (bleach) solution strong enough to destroy the spore may also destroy the embryo.

LEFT *Aerangis biloba*, like many African species, is an orchid that will succeed in a pot but often does better on a plaque mount.

So the pod is externally sterilized, and cut with a sterile blade in a sterile environment, allowing the naturally sterile seed to be sown (spread) on agar jelly in a glass (or maybe plastic) flask. The jelly contains the right mix of nutrients in exactly the right strength and has also been sterilized in the flask, usually in an autoclave. The capped flask may now be removed to an ordinary, non-sterile environment, kept at an appropriate temperature, given the right light, and kept in correct humidity. This is a sown flask.

The sterile environment for seed sowing is usually provided by working inside a glove-box. Professionals use a sterile cabinet (laminar flow cabinet) kept above atmospheric pressure by air blown in through a filter fine enough to take out even floating spores.

After a period of anything between a month and many years, the surface of the agar begins to green with minute dots as individual seeds start to absorb nutrients and begin to produce chlorophyll. Presently each dot will begin to swell to form a protocorm, which has to reach the size of the head of a match before shoots emerge to form the first leaf and also the first roots.

If a mold grows, a spore got in despite all the efforts, and the seed is lost. Even if not, and experts in well-equipped labs have a very low contamination rate, the germination rate can vary enormously. There may be only one seedling in a flask, or they may be terribly overcrowded. Even if the happy mean is achieved, and there is an appropriate number, sooner or later they will have to be taken out of the flask, and placed in another one (again all done in sterile conditions) so as to space out the little seedlings and grow them on until they are big enough to face the world on their own. This is called re-plating, and may be done several times.

A hobbyist who buys a flask of seedlings ready to come out into the world should be looking for seedlings that are all green, have no dead leaves, are not overcrowded, and are preferably at least 1½ inches high, or leaf-span. The bigger the seedlings the better.

The seedlings are removed from a glass flask by wrapping it in several layers of newspaper and gently tapping with a hammer to break the glass so that the shards can be picked off. Attempts to pluck the seedlings out through the top of the flask only damage them. By the way the "flask" may be a jar, a bottle, a box, or any other container. The early workers used expensive lab glassware Ehrlenmayer flasks, and the name is still used even when the jelly has been put into a re-used and sterilized jam jar.

The seedlings are best not separated, for this too is likely to damage them. They can be held under a faucet to wash off as much jelly as possible and then placed in a pot on top of the orchid compost (seedling compost, which is relatively fine grain), sprayed with a fungicide as a protection against infection at this late stage, and covered with a clear propagator top. A very good way of dealing with them at this stage is to water them (fungicide can be used for this), drain well, seal the propagator top to the pot with duct tape, and place the pot in a suitable environment – the orchid growing room perhaps – choosing a spot that is well lit and warm. Then the pot is left for the seedlings to grow.

This is the really hard part because they have to be left alone for weeks and months! The pot should be left sealed and the seedlings watched until they have perhaps doubled in size. No, the tape is not taken off to water them. They are not watered! Water vapor will condense on the inside of the propagator and run down back into the compost. So the water (mostly) goes around and around. During this time, which may be 8 –26 weeks, the seedlings grow a new set of roots. The roots they grew in agar jelly are not of much use to them out in the real world. As they produce new roots, so they will grow.

Finally they are ready to come out. First, take off the tape and then leave them for a few days. Next, crack open the joint between propagator lid and pot and leave them for a few more days. This allows the seedlings to adjust to the atmosphere in the orchid room. Finally, take off the top and treat the pot as a community pot of seedlings.

Repot at intervals, and on each occasion attempt to disentangle the roots so as to separate the seedlings. It gets easier as the plants enlarge. When separated, continue to keep them all together in a single community pot until they have doubled in size again, and then they will be ready to be singled up. From there on, the compost gets nearer to the standard (adult orchid) compost at each repotting, as the plants get toward, and finally reach, flowering size. What a thrill that is when your own home-raised seedlings start to flower!

Some orchids, such as some paphs, can be raised from flask to first flowering in well under two years by the hobbyist, but this is an exception. The great "plant factories" in Taiwan, Thailand, and the Netherlands, raising millions of orchids for the homes of the world, can beat this for many other plants, but use extremely sophisticated growing rooms equipped with apparatus far beyond the dream of any but the most ambitious hobbyist. Moreover, each grows large batches of a very few different orchids as compared to the ordinary amateur orchid grower who, if there are a hundred orchids in the collection likely has one hundred different kinds.

Generally speaking most growers will be content to increase their stock by one or both of two alternative means, although it merely increases the number of plants and not the variety.

The first and most obvious means is division. To be divisible, a plant must have two "leads," which means it produces new growths at two different points on the same plant. Ideally, the plant has had these two leads for some years, so that if simply cut or broken at the point where the two diverge, each piece will consist of at least two or three years growth. Such a division can be made at repotting time. Whether to do it at all is another matter. If the flowering plants are arranged in a group with a few foliage plants to hide the pots, will two separate pots each with one flower spike look any better than one pot with two spikes? Some plants certainly produce better spikes when left undivided, particularly species that tend to flower in due season, because all of the flowers which are likely will come at the same time. But some hybrids flower (instead) when a growth has reached a particular point, and if new growths come in succession, so does completion and so do flowers. A large pot with only a single flower spike may not make much of a show, and the fact that it does so every month or two may not be consolation. In such a case, it may be thought better to divide and then have a series of small pots each bearing a spike and each making a worthwhile show. But this is all in the mind of the owner, and an individual choice.

Plants can and, in some cases should, be encouraged to produce additional growths. This is true for cattleyas, where there is a length of rhizome between each two cane-like bulbs. If the rhizome is part-cut through, not enough to sever the parts, but through the outer skin, older bulbs behind the cut may then produce new growths, allowing division at some later date.

Just one or two orchids can be propagated by something akin to cuttings. Thunias, for example, can have the plump canes cut into lengths and laid on moist moss, and little plants will develop from the nodes. These are actually keikis. *Keiki* is a Hawaian word, now part of the orchid language worldwide. It is used for little plants that develop somewhere on an orchid and positively invite being removed as a complete, albeit originally miniature, replica of the parent. Dendrobiums do this a lot. Some phalaenopsis do it occasionally, and various other species in many genera do it rather more rarely. The general rule is, wait for roots to develop, and when there are two or three – each a couple of inches long – break the little plantlet off, or cut it off and apply some powder (an insecticide would do but sulfur would be ideal) to the cuts to avoid rot, pot up, and treat as a little seedling. Dendrobiums, given appropriate culture, especially hydroculture, can flower within a year of this.

There is one other propagation technique. It is important to understand it, although it is not one that an amateur hobbyist is likely to be able to practice. This is tissue propagation, which produces what are often called meristems.

ABOVE Thunia plantlets growing from nodes on old canes cut into lengths laid on moss

Everyone knows that most green plants can be propagated by taking cuttings. Keen horticulturalists will know that there are many kinds: root cuttings, where new complete plants can be grown from short lengths of root, as with some primulas; leaf cuttings where new plants can be grown, for example, by laying a leaf on a suitable compost and pinning it down (this works with some begonias); tip cuttings, where a short length of stem with a few leaves is cut from the end of a growth (that works with a large number of plants, including such warm-growing flowering plants as pelargonium and fuchsia); and inter-nodal cuttings used for clematis. But none of these techniques work with orchids. If, for example, root or leaf material is grown, even on agar jelly, in sterile conditions so that mold does not spoil the plant material, the cells may grow and multiply, but they will be specialized cells of the same kind as the material forming the starting point, and incapable of producing any other kind of cells. Leaf cells will grow new leaf cells, but never start a root or a flowering shoot.

ABOVE *Vuylstekeara* Cambria "Plush" FCC/RHS – at one time the world's most frequently seen orchid!

However there are a few cells close to the very growing point of the plant that have not yet specialized; these form the meristem of the plant. If surgically excised (cut out) and grown under sterile conditions they will multiply. The few cells will form a protocorm, which behaves just like a protocorm formed by a germinating seed, forming roots and a shoot and growing into a plant.

However, a breakthrough came with the discovery that if the protocorms are prevented from "learning" the directions up and down by slowly turning the sterile flasks in which they are growing (tumbling them), the mass of unspecialized cells will continue to grow and multiply, and can be cut into pieces, and the process repeated maybe *ad infinitum*. When gravity is allowed to have its way because the tumbling stops, the separate pieces, each a small mass of cells, start to behave like conventional protocorms again.

In the cutting up and repetition of the growing and tumbling steps, the multiplication rate of protocorms can be enormous. Not tens, or hundreds, or thousands, but much larger quantities of genetically identical protocorms, and in due course plants, can be created. It is now commonplace for commercial breeders of new orchids to make a hybrid seedpod, raise a batch of seedlings conventionally, and "flower them out" to see what is produced. They then select the plant or plants for meristem reproduction, maybe choosing a particular shade or color, or selecting a plant for flowering particularly early or late in the season, or some other commercially desirable values. They take meristem cells from those particular plants, and go on to produce a batch of 25,000 identical plants, all of which are quite indistinguishable from one another and from the parent plant. It is of course this kind of mass production, with the enormous simplification that comes from growing on a large batch of genetically identical plants, all of the same age, that has slashed production costs and made orchids available at a tiny percentage of the prices of yesteryear.

In the extreme, it is said that one million plants a year are produced of one single clone (*Vuylstekeara* Cambria var. Plush FCC/RHS), which is a hybrid incorporating genes from no less than six species – one miltoniopsis, one cochlioda, and four odontoglossum. In this particular instance, the meristemming process carried out on one and the same plant and its supposedly identical progeny for 30 years has led to a few mutations that have been found desirable in their own right – an orange form and a yellow form among them. But it does seem that plants produced most recently have not grown as strongly as divisions from the original plant did when they were marketed long before meristemming was invented and developed. So maybe the multiplication process can be carried too far with irretrievable loss of vigor. But Cambria is, in any case, a most unusual example. There is such a flood of novelty breeding and so many orchids available for mass production that it is rare for the same plant to be on offer for more than a very few years before the producers switch to something different. (And this is another illustration of why it is not useful to produce a shopping list of particular orchid hybrids, unless they are ones only marketed very recently. Older ones will almost certainly have been replaced – it would be like searching auto dealers for a new, unused Ford Model T).

BELOW *Odontoglossum bictoniense* (now called a lemboglossum) "Lyoth Pearl" AM/RHS – rare example of a very fine cultivar of a species, both awarded, and now meristemmed, and made available. Without that, there would only ever be one plant of it.

pests and diseases

Fortunately, orchids are extraordinarily tough plants and have very few pests to worry the hobbyist. Often enough, the pests in the garden are unused to orchids and will not bother them. But in the tropics there are pests that are used to orchids, and sometimes they are introduced with a recent purchase and need attention before they spread to all the collection.

Bugs, creepy-crawlies, and pests in general can be divided into two categories: Those that eat roots, leaves, or worse, the buds or flowers, and those that suck the sap. The latter category is less obvious, but cause more damage in the long term since they weaken the whole plant. An orchid that has its flower spike damaged by a slug will grow a new flower spike next year, and maybe even this year, but a plant infested by red spider may be so weak that it dies even after it has been cleaned up.

Let us deal with sapsuckers first. Scale insect is difficult to recognize as an insect at all, except by the entomologist. There are several kinds. One is a small brown lump, smaller than the head of a match, usually on the underside of leaves, often on the center rib or at the edges of the leaf. They move, but so slowly as to seem immobile, and are so firmly attached to the leaf that they do not easily wipe off. Smaller ones are often flat, as the name scale insect suggests, and of smaller sizes and paler colors. With all pests, the first step is physical removal – by wiping them with a pad of absorbent cotton soaked in denatured alcohol, which dissolves their waxy protective coat, enables easy removal, and incidentally pickles them at the same time.

Mealybug is a downy or fluffy insect, only slowly mobile, often with what looks like a protruding snout at one end – this is the long-tailed variant. They molt as they grow, leaving their old skins on the leaves like ghosts of where they have been. This one is particularly difficult because it spends part of the time hiding in the compost, or even outside the pots, so that removing just the visible ones is insufficient unless repeated quite frequently. When found, mealybug are another candidate for the absorbent cotton pad/denatured alcohol treatment.

Aphids, greenfly, and similar insects often proliferate on flower spikes, and if left unchecked will utterly destroy the buds before ever a flower is seen. Very gentle wiping with soapy water is called for here, lest the wiping action itself damages the buds.

Some hobbyists swear by neem oil, which works in two ways. It is used diluted with a fair volume of water and then sprayed, as instructed on the bottle. As the diluent water dries out, the gummy oil blocks the tiny apertures through which the bugs take in air, suffocating them. The oil also acts as an insecticide. But opinions vary, and experts now say that there are two kinds of product sold under the same name, and while one works, the other does not. How to tell the difference remains unknown!

Using a systemic insecticide, applied according to the instructions on the bottle, can destroy all of these sapsuckers. It is taken into the sap of the orchid and then ingested by the insects as they feed. This is ideal, providing the strain that is present is not resistant to that particular chemical. And since the most potent and poisonous chemicals for dealing with resistant strains tend to be barred for home use it does make life difficult. This is another reason for using physical removal as the first step. If the problem persists, try anything you can find in your supply store. Here it really is worth trying any product marked "new" or "newly introduced," since you may find something that the bugs are not yet immune to, and therefore get a chance to use it before it becomes prescribed.

Mites are not a serious problem outside the tropics, apart from one present in temperate regions, sometimes very widespread as a minor pest of apple trees. This is red spider, otherwise known as false spider mite. It is not a spider, but if the infestation is serious there is a kind of web produced on the surface of the underside of the leaves, which has led to the name. The mites are very tiny – only dots to the naked eye – and a sharp eye at that. Their presence is more often detected by a characteristic yellow mottling on the upper side of the leaves, caused by the many punctures made in the sap sucking process. If in doubt, wipe the leaves with a moistened tissue. If it comes away red, that is a stain caused by the very many mites that have been wiped off. This pest is worse when the humidity is too low, and can be very bad if orchids are being grown in a well-ventilated greenhouse next to an abandoned apple orchard. It hardly ever occurs in a greenhouse or an internal orchid room, which has no ventilators opening to the outside air. In theory, insecticides do not work on mites. But maybe the mites do not know that, for practice is different from theory, and

LEFT *Masdevallia caudate* – one of the first tropical orchids to reach the Western World from South America

systemic insecticides, coupled with wiping the leaves, seem to clear up most infections of this pest.

Pill bugs, or woodlice, are not insects, but belong to another order of invertebrates. It can be difficult or impossible to convince pest experts, even at well-known horticultural advice centers, that they are any kind of problem. But hobbyists know that they can be. If exposed aerial roots are seen to have jagged ends, as if broken off, this is the likely culprit. And they also like the tender greenery of newly emerging phally leaves, which then are nibbled at the edges. They will sometimes nibble the small blue-colored metaldehyde bait intended to kill slugs and snails, but this is also poisonous to plants if allowed to remain in contact with tender leaves and must be kept clear of the plant itself. However, another way of using this bait is to stick it to a double-sided patch of Scotch tape and stick that to the plant in a place likely to be accessible to the bugs. By the way, this also works well when slugs and snails are the target.

Weevil powders made especially for that purpose can kill pill bugs. But the best and most ideal solution is to try and exclude them from the growing area. However, in a rural environment they can make their way through ventilator screens and since they are ubiquitous in gardens around, at least, the temperate world, the best that can be done is to discourage them or kill

RIGHT Lorem ipsum dolor sit amet, consectetuer adipiscing elit, sed diam Lorem ipsum dolor sit amet, consectetuer adipiscing elit, sed diam

them on sight. Discouragement can be quite effective. They do not like to walk across any of the heavy metals, and copper is especially good as a deterrent. Copper can be applied to benches, walls, and floors as a microscopic layer by spraying with one of the fungicidal copper-based compositions designed for horticultural usage. That layer, a molecule or so thick (when dry), can be effective, until washed or worn away. So, spray again when the pest returns – quite frequently in practice.

Any one particular area may have a local problem. If you are next to agricultural areas growing fields of cabbages, white fly can be a pest. If you are near horticultural areas growing flowers in polythene tunnels, thrips can be a pest, and so on. Whatever control is used could be tried most cautiously on an orchid –- and if there is no harm to the plant, then maybe used more widely. Unfortunately anti-pest chemicals very rarely give advice in relation to orchids, perhaps because of consumer law and the fear of claims for damages. They have also probably not been tested on orchids by the makers because the cost of testing would be disproportionate to the likely value of sales in such a specialized area.

Slug and snails are pests in many parts of the world. Just one of them can do an awful lot of damage, and while a plant is unlikely to be killed, the leaves may be marred so that the plant becomes unshowable, or a flower spike may be quite eaten through, and one season's blooms lost. If you inspect the collection very regularly, remember that a snail or slug often has a meal and rests up locally, in order to return to the same plant for its next dinner. Looking very closely around the pot rim, under the pot, and in places near a damaged plant may result in successful location. They usually like to start feeding as dusk falls, and consequently an evening visit with a flashlight is the best time to catch them. Rubber gloves are recommended for the squeamish, and indeed do consider that the pests have crawled over the ground somewhere, and may have picked up goodness knows what. Indeed, rubber gloves are recommended for all greenhouse/orchid rooms/cultural operations.

RIGHT *Encyclia ciliare*

Slug bait can be applied (see pill bugs), and the copper trick is also effective against slugs and snails.

The most recently mentioned anti-slug and snail treatment is coffee. It appears that the dregs from the coffee pot are likely to be fatal to these pests, and may not harm orchids. But at the time of writing, this is a new report so far untested in the hobbyist world, and the use of coffee for this purpose is to be approached with caution

Viruses do exist in plants. They seem to be more talked about than proven, but if suspected it is best to incinerate the suspect plant rather than risk infection spreading. Most known orchid viruses manifest themselves in distorted flowers, but these can also come from cultural stress. In any case, if a plant flowers with distorted blossoms two years running it should certainly be destroyed. The other well-known or discussed virus manifestation is in black streaked leaves, the streaks being discontinuous or broken. The streaks can certainly be provoked in cymbidiums if they are grown in overly cold conditions. If the streaks can be "grown out" (meaning not visible), in new growths under better conditions, they can again be taken as a sign of stress. However, if they are still there, the cymbidium virus may be the cause. Another symptom of the virus is that the plants do not flower (readily), so a non-flowering plant with black streaks is a certain candidate for the flames. Orchid viruses are spread by using cutting tools without sterilization (flaming or alcohol are the techniques to avoid problems, but alcohol seems less certain) and also of course by sap-sucking insect pests moving from one plant to another.

Other black spots, which can be seen to be dead tissue, are sometimes found on phalaenopsis leaves. They are usually due to a bacterial infection. Plants grown too wet, too humid (especially), and too dark are very prone to this. There is no cure, although drying up the wet spot is a must, and almost any fine powder will do. The powdered cinnamon used in the kitchen is excellent for drying up cut surfaces of plants and can also be used here. Since it comes from the bark of the cinnamon tree, which has natural insecticidal properties to stop insects boring into the living tree, it may find other uses too.

RIGHT *Burrageara* Living Fire "Glowing Embers" is an odontoglossum-derived hybrid

rots and molds

Rots and molds in general are often due to plant stress, even if a specific name can be given to the bacteria. Overfeeding can scorch roots, making plants more susceptible, and overhead watering with fertilizer solution, allowing the fertilizer to remain in the crown of the plant overnight, encourages the bacteria to breed. Plants in the wild – always "watered" (rained upon) from overhead – are never found with crown rot, but that is pure water not fertilizer. The moral is, when watering plants in a way which may allow water to collect in the crown, either use pure water, or if a fertilizer solution is used, then end up with enough water on its own to flush out any remaining fertilizer. Or, of course, add some disinfectant to the water – Physan is an excellent all-purpose one for orchids. If the collection is in more tropical conditions, then Phytan may be used. Both should be obtainable from a hobbyists supply store.

Many plants, both orchids and others, weep a sugary sap solution from their pores at certain times. Maybe the sap pressure becomes too high when the physiological processes of the plant pump the sap too fast for it to be used and the pressure is relieved this way. The sugar is attractive to ants and other insects, and is an ideal place for mold spores to germinate and grow into unsightly black patches on the leaves and stems. When seen, these can be wiped off with ordinary leaf-wipes. If left on, the molds may carry on growing when the sugars are used up and create more permanent scars on the leaves. Damage of that kind is not very significant, but can never be cured or repaired, and the ideal plant is one with perfect foliage and no marks of any kind from molds or any other source. However, to keep the plants looking at their best it is not necessary to watch over them as closely as a nursemaid watches a baby, it is likely to be enough to look over the collection of plants, say weekly, and then a quick wipe can deal with problems before they become important. As the old proverb says, "a stitch in time, saves nine."

gallery of orchids

RIGHT **Aerides odoratum**

Southeast Asian orchid of the vanda family, sometimes called "fox-brush orchids." This one has scented flowers, an inch or larger, and commonly 50+ per spike. Needs warmer conditions, and like all vandas, good humidity.

LEFT **Aerangis luteo-alba**

An East African orchid, quite diminutive, even a large plant with several growths and carrying a dozen sprays of flowers will fit in a 4 inch pot. Wants intermediate rather shady conditions and good humidity.

ABOVE **Angraecum germinyanum**

Another African orchid. Can quickly grow into quite a bush with its freely branching habit. The white flowers typical of angraecums generally, are night scented and with a long spur.

ABOVE **Baptista echinata**

Called the bumble bee orchid, but it needs a close-up of a single flower to see why. Needs the same treatment as odontoglossum and other thin-leaved cool/intermediate orchids – high humidity, moderate or less light. A good specimen can have very many flowers but is a challenge to the grower.

BELOW
Epidendrum radicans

One of the reed-stem epidendrums. Flowers at the top of a cane no thicker than a pencil and maybe 3 feet high. Will flower for months or even years, and produce both new growths from the base and keikis (pot them up to make new plants) quite freely.

ABOVE *Ascocenda* Khun Nok "Nakathun"

Vandaceous orchids can be meristemmed too, and this one has been – it is usually the best hybrids which are chosen for this treatment – there is no point in propagating second best! Intermediate, bright light, but not full sun.

ABOVE LEFT *Barkeria skinneri*

High light plants from Mexico. Live on very little, and dislike being potted. One way is to treat them the way the Thai treat vandas – bare root, no compost, and spray daily when in active growth.

BELOW *Arundina bambusaefolia*

Grown in tropical gardens and parks all round the world. The picture shows plants growing wild on the edge of a drainage ditch in a Costa Rican lane. Can be flowered in an orchid house, in which case intermediate or warm, shady and damp.

ABOVE *Bifrenaria harrisoniae*

In the UK they call this an "old orchid" – meaning popular a hundred years ago – There was then a Prime Minister who was a great orchid fan and always wore an orchid in the button-hole of his tail-coat – and this was one of his favorites. Flowers 2 to 3 inches across, waxy, lightly scented. Intermediate conditions.

ABOVE *Masdevallia xanthina*

The section of the genus including this plant was once common around Macchu Picchu in Peru, but may now be almost extinct from over-collecting. Its closest relatives are red – *M. coccinea*, but many other-colored close relatives exist. Some hobbyists major on them.

RIGHT *Oneidium lanceanum*

This is a warm-growing, light-loving oncidium, with hard, sharp, rigid leaves. It is sometimes called "mule-eared" for this reason.

FAR RIGHT

Dendrobium infundibulum

A completely different kind of dendrobium with upright stouter canes, and large white flowers which last and last and last… Needs to be kept growing all through the year in shady intermediate conditions.

ABOVE *Promenea citrina*

Dislikes wet leaves. Loves moist roots. Must be well drained or will rot. The solution is to grow in sphagnum moss in a net pot, watering by careful immersion of the lower part of the pot in rainwater, and then the bright flowers hang over the edge and delight the eye.

LEFT *Dendrobium anosmum*

There are over a thousand Dendrobium species and very many are worth growing. This particular one is *D. anosmum*, with scented flowers – many people think it is reminiscent of rhubarb – and others say raspberry. This has canes which can be several feet long, arching, with thin leaves, and can flower from practically every node (leaf base) along the length of the canes. A well-grown plant with dozens of canes can be completely hidden by flowers.

BELOW *Calanthe triplicata*

Calanthe is a wide-spread genus. This one comes from the eastern part of Thailand and maybe Vietnam too. It lights up the darkest parts of the rainforest with its flowers, growing terrestrially at fairly high altitudes – meaning that it does not demand as much heat as might be thought, and certainly low light.

FAR RIGHT

Paphiopedilum

micranthum

One of the slipper orchid species discovered in China in the last 20 years.

ABOVE *Calanthe sieboldii*

This is one of the cooler growing calanthes, and may even withstand a little frost if grown in a garden bed, and covered with some litter to provide winter protection. Deciduous, flowering from new growths made in the Spring. Terrestrial, as all calanthes are, so a more peaty/leaf-moldy compost but still well drained.

BELOW *Oerstediella centradenia*

Best grown on a moss pole, as it loves to produce new growths exclusively as keikis, which prefer to have their roots mostly in the air. Small but pretty flowers, regularly produced.

ABOVE *Angulocaste* Oakdon

An intergeneric hybrid between lycaste and angloa and resembling the parent species commonly known as the "tulip orchid." Wants intermeditate conditions and a good amount of space when grown well.

LEFT *Coleogyne cristata*

White flowers up to 3 inches across, up to about 7 per spike, produced in Spring at the side of the bulb made up in the previous year. These plants quickly bulk up to produce large plants. Cool growing.

RIGHT *Coleogyne mooreana*

Cooler growing and altogether more compact – this one will branch freely and can easily have half a dozen flowering growths in quite a modest-sized pot, the flowers being 3 inches across, and pure white. More modest in its needs for heat too.

LEFT *Coelogyne pandurata*

Requires a lot of space as the bulbs can be several inches apart on a rhizome, and the pendant spray of flowers can be 18 inches, or more, long with many large flowers, but what a sight then. Needs rather more warmth than most.

RIGHT *Dendrochilum*

– the chain orchids easily form specimen plants – a six-inch pot may carry 30 or 40 or more spikes of pendant chains of flowers, individually only half an inch across, and often strongly scented. The picture shows just a tiny portion of a single chain which might have 50+ flowers in it.

LEFT *Chysis bractescens*

Another Mexican species. Large waxy flowers. Quite easy in a cool house. Has one or two more often seen relatives, having rather smaller yellow flowers, but this is a much finer plant.

LEFT *Masdevallia rubicon*

Different members of this genus live under such different conditions that it is always necessary to enquire about a particular plant, and one that looks healthy but is not flowering freely is almost certainly in the wrong temperature conditions.

RIGHT

Summer-flowering cymbidiums

Most cymbidiums flower within a month or two before the shortest day, up to 3 months after it. But these are bred from a summer-flowering species and flower in late summer. Worth looking out for, although infrequent as yet. This one is Golden Elf.

ABOVE *Stanhopea sp.*

These were grown in cultivation for many years before flowers were ever seen, because they produce their spike vertically downward, and they were getting lost in the flower pots. Grow in a basket if you want to see the remarkable, and large, flowers.

BELOW *Cattleya bowringiana*

One of the many cattleya species which have been unfairly neglected in favor of the more gaudy hybrids. Can be grown into a specimen as large as you can manage to house (and carry to shows) if wanted, growing larger bulbs with ever bigger heads of finer flowers, the longer it is kept growing well and undisturbed.

ABOVE

Odontonia Boussole "Blanche"

This plant was meristemmed in the early days of the technique (*circa* 1970) but is so easily propagated from back-bulbs that it tends to crop up in small numbers at hobbyists' surplus plant sales as well as at the smaller specialist hobby nursery. Well worth looking out for. Easily double-spikes on each growth.

index

useful addresses and acknowledgments

If you are now hooked on orchids, why not join your local orchid society? You are sure of a welcome and, among other things, you will gain access to help, quite probably a library, and also a source of plants at prices much lower than you would pay in a store – from other members' divisions and propagations. Orchid Societies are usually very friendly places.

To find your nearest in USA, contact the American Orchid Society at: American Orchid Society, 16700 AOS Lane, Delray Beach, Florida 33446-4351.

In UK, your contact is: British Orchid Council, Secretary Mr E.S. Manning, Estover, 25a Forest Road, Tarporley, Cheshire CW6 0HX.

For a complete listing of Orchid Societies In Australia go to www.orchidsonline.com.au. Find Internet orchid clubs at www.orchid-talk.co.uk.

All photography by the author. All of the plants shown, with very few exceptions, are or were grown and owned by the author.